AI and IA:
Utopia or Extinction?

Edited by Ted Peters

AI and IA:
Utopia or Extinction?

Edited by Ted Peters

Adelaide
2018

Agathon: A Journal of Ethics and Value in the Modern World
Volume 5, 2018

Agathon refers to the Greek word used by Plato in the *Republic* to refer to 'the good beyond being', most notably deployed in recent times by Iris Murdoch and Emmanuel Levinas, both of whom use this touchstone to situate ethics at the heart of all of philosophy

We live in an evolving and increasingly complex world but our ethical concepts have frequently struggled to keep pace with the change. As a result, much of what passes for public debate at present remains in the grip of either deterministic or consequentialist thinking, both built on outdated assumptions and both representing attempts to address major issues in the absence of ethical concepts. We suffer, as Iris Murdoch lamented, a 'loss of concepts, the loss of a moral and political vocabulary'.

The interdisciplinary journal, *agathon*, seeks to bring together scholars from across the humanities, social sciences and sciences, including disciplines such as philosophy, theology, law and medicine, to engage with the ethical questions that now beset the modern world..

The journal is a home for considering questions such as how we deal with competing values in ethical discourse, how ethical theory finds expression in practice, what constitutes ethical character and how it is cultivated, and what excellence and wisdom look like for the ethical person or society in the twenty-first century.

Agathon is an international and interdisciplinary refereed journal published annually by ATF Press.

Chief Editor
Dr Paul Babie, University of Adelaide Law School Professor of the Theory and Law of Property

Editorial Board
• Professor Terence Lovat, Editor in Chief Bonhoeffer Legacy, The University of Newcastle, Australia & Hon Fellow University of Oxford, UK.
• Professor Robert Crotty, former Director, Ethics Centre of South Australia, Emeritus Professor of Religion and Education, University of South Australia, Adelaide.
• Managing Editor and Publisher Mr Hilary Regan, Publisher, ATF Press Publishing Group, PO Box 234 Brompton, SA 5007, Australia. Email: hdregan@atf.org.au

Subscription Rates
Local: Individual Aus $55 Institutions Aus $65 Overseas: Individuals US $60 Institutions US $65

Agathon is published by ATF Press an imprint of the ATF Press Publishing Group which is owned by ATF (Australia) Ltd (ABN 90 116 359 963) and is published once a year. ISSN 2201-3563

ISBN: 978-1-925679-20-5   soft
         978-1-925679-21-2   hard
         978-1-925679-22-9   epub
         978-1-925679-23-6   pdf

Published by:

An imprint of the ATF Press Publishing Group owned by ATF (Australia) Ltd.
PO Box 504
Hindmarsh, SA 5007
ABN 90 116 359 963
www.atfpress.com
Making a lasting impact

Table of Contents

Human Utopia or Human Extinction?

Ted Peters

'As AI becomes invisibly ubiquitous, new ethical challenges emerge. The protection of human self-determination is one of the most relevant concerns and must be addressed urgently.'
– Mariarosaria Taddeo and Luciano Floridi[1]

The fast-moving frontier of Artificial Intelligence (AI) in league with Intelligence Amplification (IA) prompt anxiety in some quarters. When it comes to smart phones or autonomous gadgets for vacuuming our living room carpets, a brief moment of 'wow' is quickly superseded by 'oh, hum.' Robotic intelligence, though initially fascinating, seems to prompt no worries about the short-range future. But, what about the long-range future? When we forecast the evolution of post-human superintelligence that will either bring a technological utopia or render *Homo sapiens* extinct, anxiety causes us to ask existential questions. In this issue of *Ethics,* we ask those questions.

Could the techie whizzes among us invent enough gadgets to relieve human beings from the drudgery of work? Can we look forward to a near future where robots and sex-bots and nanny-bots and chef-bots and mow-the-lawn-bots provide everything we previously had to strive for? Could we create our own utopia? Or, might there be a risk that the AI we create will, like the Sorcerer's Apprentice, get out of control? Might the superintelligent children of our technological procreation discard their parents as outdated junk? Will AI and IA bring us to a fork in the road where one route leads to utopia and the other to extinction?

---

1. Mariarosaria Taddeo and Luciano Floridi, 'How AI Can be a Force for Good', in *Science*, 361/6404 (24 August 2018): 751–752, at 751.

We pause here to ask: what is intelligence anyway? Could *Homo sapiens* with moderate intelligence give birth to a post-human species of more intelligent hybrids, cyborgs, or robots? If we humans are able to create cybernetic geniuses as our progeny, will we the creators attain the status of technological gods? Could *we* humans advance to the status of *Homo Deus?* Or, because that race of superintelligent and super-powerful creatures will survive us, should we designate *them* as 'gods'? Will we creatures have created a divine race to surpass us? Will the post-human discard us mere humans as obsolete trash?

These questions raise the specter of transhumanism. 'The field of artificial intelligence is deeply rooted in transhumanist visions for the future', avers Natasha Vita-More, Executive Director of Humanity + Incorporated.[2]

Like riding a jet propelled escalator, the transhumanists (abbreviated H+) among us are rocketing evolution toward an unprecedented new stage, namely, superintelligence. Whether through deep brain implants to amplify existing human intelligence (IA) or through creating robots with artificial intelligence (AI), a new posthuman species is scheduled to emerge. The event of posthuman emergence is dubbed, the *Singularity.* After crossing the Singularity threshold, superintelligence will take the reins of evolution and continue the advance to yet higher levels of intelligence until all of reality has been imbued with the cyber mind. Among other vicissitudes to be conquered is death, which will be surpassed by radical life extension or even cybernetic immortality. The transhumanists offer us a utopian vision of cosmic consciousness, even if we atavistic *Homo sapiens* may not be there to enjoy it.

These forecasts should give theologians pause, especially when it comes to anthropology and eschatology. Are the presuppositions about human nature adopted by transhumanists accurate? Is disembodied intelligence the same intelligence we in human bodies have come to know? Is the concept of whole brain emulation leading to cybernetic immortality realistic? Is the eschatological vision of the transhumanist compatible with, or contradictory to, the biblical promise of the Kingdom of God?

Some theologians, such as D Gareth Jones, warn of a competition between saviors. Who will save us? Science or Christ? 'The excesses

---

2. Natasha Vita-More, *Transhumanism: What is it?* (published by author, 2018). 64.

of transhumanism with its picture of a new world order, in which medicine will be devoted to conquering mortality, overcoming ageing, vanquishing neurodegenerative diseases and enabling people to live to 600 or so years of age as healthy and fulfilled individuals, rightly repel Christians....These extreme vistas represent a rerun of the science-as-saviour mentality.'[3] Or, to put the issue in First Commandment terms, does the H+ veneration of technology tempt us to idolatry, tempt us to revere the progress of science as salvific?

Agathon Articles

In the articles to follow here in this edition of *Ethics*, we will ask whether the disjunction between utopia and extinction provides the most realistic set of alternatives. According to Alan Weissenbacher, book review editor for *Theology and Science,* there is no reason to think that development of AI or IA will represent anything dramatic at all, especially once one assesses critically several of the assumptions that lead some futurists to overenthusiastic optimism. In his contribution 'Artificial Intelligence and Intelligence Amplification: Salvation, Extinction, Faulty Assumptions, and Original Sin', Weissenbacher analyses three questionable assumptions made by techno-optimists and transhumanists. First, the definition of intelligence we find in AI and IA technology is vague and confused. Wet brain human intelligence and dry machine intelligence are so different, they cannot rightly be compared. They are two different things, even if they functionally overlap at times.

Second, according to Weissenbacher, there appears to be an implicit assumption especially among transhumanists that higher intelligence equates to greater morality. This assumption, every theologian knows, is clearly false. Some of the brightest minds in history have devised and disguised the most horrendous evils. There is no relationship between enhanced intelligence and enhanced morality.

Third, closely related to this is the assumption that greater intelligence will bring with it the will to address societal problems. This is by no means the case. One could easily forecast that the generation of human beings who initiates the era of superintelligence could use

---

3. D Gareth Jones, 'A Christian Perspective on Human Enhancement', in *Science and Christian Belief,* 22/2 (2010): 14–16, at 14.

this newfound power for greedy or tyrannical purposes. Technological advance does not entail moral advance.

Unless, of course, you're Mark Graves. Graves, currently pursuing research at the University of Notre Dame in the US, is author of 'AI Reading Theology: Promises and Perils'. Graves is both a computer scientist and a theologian who raises the question: should we ask AI to read and interpret theology, especially the theology of St. Thomas Aquinas. Given the current computational ability to analyze and generate theological text, reasonably near future AI may plausibly read theology comparable to a first-year seminary student and have the capacity to learn more. Should theologians contribute to AI learning theology? Yes. Benefits include technologically enhanced theological interpretations and, note, improved AI morality. AI reasoning necessarily entails moral reasoning, he says. Really? I find this doubtful, frankly, because AI does not include selfhood; and it takes selfhood for a sense of moral responsibility and culpability. Be that as it may, Graves invitation for AI to enter the very heart of theological and ethical deliberation is both unique and exciting.

Asking a computer to reason morally would be to ask too much, according to Noreen Herzfeld, a hybrid theologian and computer science professor. Herzfeld fears that too much hype is leading us to unrealistic expectations. Despite nearly three quarters of a century of research, to date no electronic device yet invented exhibits intelligence. Computers compute, to be sure; but they cannot pass the Turing Test. They are not intelligent. Even though it's too early to predict what will happen in the future, Herzfeld bets that authentic machine intelligence remains science fiction. In her article, "The Enchantment of Artificial Intelligence," Herzfeld suggests that the H+ vision is extravagant, unrealistic. Even if Weissenbacher and Herzfeld are correct about long range forecasts, however, AI developments will have implications in the near future for human work and human dignity.

Despite our enchantment with AI, IA, and the H+ vision, all this might be considered dystopian rather than utopian. According to Australian barrister Neville Rochow, such dystopias are familiar to us. But, rather than focus on the technology associated with Amazon, Apple, Facebook, and Google plus the horizon of new AI advances, Rochow worries about the business side of technology. In his contribution, 'Somnambulating Towards AI Dystopia? The Future of Rights and Freedoms', Rochow says history teaches that supranational corporations cannot be trusted with unchecked power. Corporations do not respect human rights. No one can predict the effect AI will have on human rights. We should take our rights seriously before the bio-technological lottery begins. Prompt international action is required to regulate AI developers and corporations.

'Faith creates the self in human beings.' Following Paul Tillich, Dan Peterson recognizes the decisive role played by faith in human personhood and then applies it to Strong AI. If AI is ever to equal the human level of intelligence, it will need to acquire both personhood and faith. We can anticipate what this looks like if we watch fictional robots on the big screen. Peterson offers a delightful exegesis of R2-D2 in *Star Wars: A New Hope* and K2-SO in *Rogue One: A Star Wars Story*. Peterson shows how faith as a capacity would be indispensible if Strong AI is ever to attain *imago Hominis*. In this essay, Peterson provides an excellent example of how a theologian can contribute to the creative mutual interaction between science and theology.

Shakespeare exclaims rhetorically: 'What a piece of work is man! How noble in reason! how infinite in faculties! in form and moving, how express and admirable! in action how like an angel! in apprehension, how like a god!' Now, are we talking about the humanity we know? Or, are we talking about the post-human that artificial intelligence and intelligence amplification could bring into existence? Will this amount to what is truly human, or what is post-human?

Martinez Hewlett, evolutionary biologist and fiction author, poses these questions in his article, 'What a Piece of Work is Man: On Being and Becoming Human in Science Fiction'. Hewlett interrogates science fiction, because there the question of what it means to be a human person is brought into sharp focus. Hewlett selects three authors whose work has influenced the genre and has been the inspiration for film adaptations: Isaac Asimov (*I, Robot*), Philip K Dick (*Blade Runner*), and Richard K. Morgan (*Altered Carbon*). All three challenge us by pushing the limits of robotics, androids, and mind uploading. They scenario visions of what the future might be in the wake of technological advances in artificial intelligence. Who shall we become?

In his article, 'Idle Hands and the Omega Point: Labor Automation and Roman Catholic Social Teaching', theologian and ethicist Levi Checketts assesses the impact of AI on work. Will AI replace work? He examines three polar theologies of work present in Roman

Catholic thought: labor as drudgery, labor as dignified calling, and labor as an obstacle. These three theologies inform an eschatological vision of labor—Christians are called to work to build the kingdom of God, not merely to acquire material possessions. What might be the implications for the distribution of resources and the problem of idleness in a post-labor world. All of this suggests Catholics must promote a future of dignified labor dedicated to love of neighbor and God.

In my own article, 'Artificial Intelligence, Transhumanism, and Frankenfear', I argue that even if AI (beyond rapid computation and cute gadgets) never comes to pass, theologians must speculate with transhumanist visionaries about the prospect of superintelligence, about the prophesied extinction of *Homo sapiens,* and about the survival of a post-human species. While advances in AI technology that benefit humanity should be celebrated, extravagant utopian promises should be met with a healthy dose of Frankenfear, that is, caution. AI and IA advances in the near future may very well make life on Earth for human beings and even the ecosphere better; yet the more extravagant utopian promises for the long-range future could risk large scale destruction.

Intelligence versus Love

Utopian promises beyond the Singularity threshold are unrealistic on two counts. The first is anthropological. To surmise that this generation of human beings could create a superior intelligence—where the creature is more intelligent than the creator—defies the logic of plausibility. Yes, we human beings have created power tools that are stronger than we who designed and manufactured them. This is a positive precedent. Yet, intelligence seems to require more than mere design. Because intelligence as we experience it in ourselves and certain animals requires both the capacity for insight and for decision-making, it's difficult to imagine that superintelligence could be the product of a design. It's difficult to imagine that what is designed would be more intelligent than the designer.

From the perspective of the Christian theologian, intelligence is a curious category. Why does it rise to the top of the values list for transhumanists? Why is it the trump card which defines the desirable future? For the follower of Jesus, love belongs on top of the values list, not intelligence. To the children--not to the technological whizzes--belongs the kingdom of God, said Jesus. 'Let the little children come to me; do not stop them; for it is to such as these that the kingdom of God belongs' (Mk 10:14). With the logic of intelligence presupposed by H+, could H+ apply their technology to the capacity to love? Could we procreate a future generation of creatures more dedicated than we to love, compassion, healing, and peace? As laudable as increased intelligence might be, it should not sit atop our list of values.

The second unrealistic assumption made by H+ has to do with eschatology. Transhumanists assume that evolution is progressive. Plus they assume that increased intelligence leads to increased moral resolve. A more intelligent superspecies, H+ assumes, will have the moral capacity to heal all psychological, sociological, and ecological ills so that all consciousness can enjoy a higher level tranquility and even harmony. Yet, I ask: can a leopard change its spots? Can a sinful human race beget progeny healed of their sin without an act of divine grace? To assume that an increase in intelligence leads automatically to an increase in moral will is fallacious. It defies history, experience, and theological insight.

The ultimate transformation Christians look forward to is eschatological. It will be a gift of divine grace. It would behoove the present generation to view AI advance as penultimate, not ultimate. A healthy dose of caution is warranted.

Conclusion

In treating our theme, 'AI and IA: Human Utopia or Human Extinction?' this edition of *Ethics* engages in public theology. *Public theology*, I believe, should be *conceived in the church, reflected on critically in the academy, and addressed to the world for the sake of the world.*[4] Public theology has five tasks: pastoral, apologetic, scientific, political, and prophetic tasks. The writers of theme articles in this volume are taking up the task of engaging science and technology from a theological perspective.

---

4. Ted Peters, 'Public Theology: Its Pastoral, Apologetic, Scientific, Political, and Prophetic Tasks', in *International Journal of Public Theology*, 12/2 (2018): 153–177; https://brill.com/abstract/journals/ijpt/12/1/ijpt.12.issue-1.xml.

Readers should take away two significant points. First, God created the human species to be creative; and the future of science and technology represents the *imago Dei* at work within history. Second, because scientific and technological advance occur within history, we should avoid asking for more than it can deliver. No scientific insight or technological innovation can accomplish what God's promise of new creation can deliver. The wisdom of Reinhold Niebuhr abides today as well as it did three quarters of a century ago. 'The Christian hope of consummation of life and history is less absurd than alternate doctrines which seek to comprehend and to effect the completion of life by some power or capacity inherent in man and his history.'[5] When comparing the transhumanist promise with the biblical promise, the latter is less preposterous.

---

5. Reinhold Niebuhr, *The Nature and Destiny of Man*, Gifford Lectures, 2 Volumes (New York, Scripbners, 1941) 2:298.

The Enchantment of Artificial Intelligence

Noreen Herzfeld

'Against utopianism the Christian faith insists that the final consummation of history lies beyond the conditions of the temporal process. Against other-worldliness it asserts that the consummation fulfills rather than negates the historical process.'
– Reinhold Niebuhr[1]

Abstract. Does the advance of AI technology promise utopia? Or does it pose an existential risk to human life on Earth as we know it? Fears of a super-intelligent robot apocalypse may be premature, yet we dare not hope for more benefits than AI technology can actually deliver. AI will disrupt (1) the economy; (2) politics; and (3) our private lives. Mindless programs will overtake many of our currently mindless jobs. Data mining will give us new correlations on which we will base an increasing number of decisions, some of them leading to false premises and unjust actions. Social media and robotic sex partners will take the place of authentic face to face relationships. But AI will not tell us how to respond to these changes. Only we humans can do that.

Key Terms. Artificial Intelligence, robot, Singularity, Reinhold Niebuhr, Ray Kurzweil, Elon Musk

Bio. Noreen L Herzfeld is Nicholas and Bernice Reuter Professor of Science and Religion at the College of St. Benedict and St. John's University in Collegeville, Minnesota. She is author of *In Our Image: Artificial Intelligence and the Human Spirit* (Minneapolis: Fortress Press, 2002).

---

1. Reinhold Niebuhr, *The Nature and Destiny of Man*, Gifford Lectures, 2 Volumes (New York, Scribners, 1941). 2:291.

In July 2017 at a meeting of the National Governor's Association, Tesla founder and CEO Elon Musk issued the following warning regarding the future of artificial intelligence: 'AI is a fundamental existential risk for human civilization, and I don't think people fully appreciate that.' Claiming access to cutting-edge AI technology, Musk called for proactive government regulation, noting that while such regulation is generally 'irksome, . . . by the time we are reactive in AI regulation, it's too late . . . I think people should be really concerned about it', Musk said: 'I keep sounding the alarm bell.'[2]

Musk is not alone. Several years ago physicist Stephen Hawking told the BBC: 'The development of full artificial intelligence could spell the end of the human race.'[3] According to Hawking, AI could 'take off on its own, and re-design itself at an ever-increasing rate . . . Humans, who are limited by slow biological evolution, couldn't compete, and would be superseded.'[4]

This concern has been a staple of science fiction for decades (see *The Terminator* or *2001*). However, those with a more intimate knowledge of AI disagree. As MIT computer scientist Rodney Brooks has wryly pointed out, Musk and Hawking "don't work in AI themselves. For those who do work in AI, we know how hard it is to get anything to actually work through product level."[5] Virtual reality pioneer and Microsoft resident guru Jaron Lanier says anyone with experience of modern software should know not to worry about our future robotic overlords. 'Just as some newborn race of superintelligent robots is about to consume all humanity, our dear old species will likely be saved by a Windows crash. The poor robots will linger pathetically, *begging us to reboot them*, even though they'll know it would do no good.'[6]

---

2. https://www.c-span.org/video/?431119-6/elon-musk-addresses-nga
3. https://www.bbc.co.uk/news/technology-30290540
4. https://www.bbc.co.uk/news/technology-30290540
5. Connie Loizos, 'This famous roboticist doesn't think Elon Musk understands AI', https://techcrunch.com/2017/07/19/this-famous-roboticist-doesnt-think-elon-musk-understands-ai/, accessed 9/14/18.
6. Jaron Lanier, 'One-half of a Manifesto', in *Wired*, December 1, 2000. https://www.wired.com/2000/12/lanier-2/

Who is right? Does AI pose an existential risk to humankind?[7] Not for the reasons Hawking and Musk imagine. We are unlikely to have intelligent computers that think in ways we humans think, ways as versatile as the human brain or even better, for many, many years, if ever. However, that doesn't mean we are out of the woods. 'AI' programs that do one thing and do that thing very well (think Deep Blue) are progressing by leaps and bounds and stand to undermine, or at least drastically change, our economy and our politics. In fact, they are already doing so, as seen in the 2016 American election or in predictions, such as a recent one by the McKinsey Global Institute, that in ten years up to thirty per cent of our current jobs will be altered or made obsolete by AI.[8]

Such dislocation in the workplace, coupled with the potential for social dislocation from applications as disparate as social media and sexbots challenges our perception of who we are as human beings and what we are worth. Nor does AI need to be totally successful to effect this challenge. While the dire predictions of Musk and Hawking are unlikely to unfold, the simple idea of AI enchants us, obscuring its true risks and pushing many toward a kind of magical thinking that blinds us to who and what we are, and who we, as Christians, are truly called to serve.

Why the Singularity (Probably) Won't Happen

Early AI researchers believed a machine that could solve calculus problems or play a credible game of chess would be intelligent. Today we carry such machines—our smartphones or calculators—around in our pockets every day but do not consider them particularly intelligent. Computer scientists quickly learned that many problems we consider difficult turn out to be relatively easy to program while the skills of a toddler such as emotion recognition, or traversing a crowded room, are much more difficult. However, recent advances in machine learning and sensory interpretation are starting to conquer these areas as well.

---

7. An existential risk is a risk of an event that would either annihilate human life on Earth or permanently and drastically curtail its potential.
8. https://www.mckinsey.com/featured-insights/future-of-organizations-and-work/Jobs-lost-jobs-gained-what-the-future-of-work-will-mean-for-jobs-skills-and-wages

The Holy Grail of AI, known as 'strong AI' or 'artificial general intelligence' (AGI) is to design a machine capable of performing any task the human brain can perform. AGI is the AI of science fiction—a machine with intelligence equal to or surpassing human intelligence. It is also the AI Elon Musk and Stephen Hawking warn us to fear.

Ever since the 1960s we have been told such an AI is just around the corner. The first flush of early successes, such as Newell and Simon's solution to the Towers of Hanoi problem[9] or Weitzenbaum's ELIZA, essentially a chat bot that mimicked a Rogerian psychologist,[10] led Carnegie Mellon professor Herbert Simon to predict in 1965 that 'machines will be capable, within twenty years, of doing any work a man can do'.[11] Similarly, MIT professor Marvin Minsky, in a 1970 interview for Life magazine, expected that '[i]n from three to eight years we will have a machine with the general intelligence of an average human being'.[12] Needless to say, these predictions were over-optimistic.[13]

In the 1980s AI researchers scaled back their expectations and produced a variety of functioning programs called 'weak AI' or expert systems, programs designed to do one and only one task. The problem with weak AI is whether it is AI at all; in other words, how can you tell what is artificial intelligence and what is simply a good computer program? A typical expert system is Deep Blue, IBM's chess playing program that, in 1997, beat then reigning world champion Gary Kasparov. Deep Blue was designed, not simply only to play chess, but only to play against Kasparov. Detractors pointed out that Kasparov went on to become a politician in his native Russia while Deep Blue was dismantled.

9. A Newell, J Shaw, H Simon, 'Report on a general problem-solving program', in *Proceedings of the International Conference on Information Processing*, 1959, 256–264.
10. Joseph Weitzenbaum, *Computer Power and Human Reason: From Judgement to Calculation* (New York: WH Freeman and Co, 1976), 7.
11. Herbert Simon, *The Shape of Automation for Men and Management* (New York: Harper & Row, 1965), 96.
12. Though Minsky now claims he was misquoted. Daniel Crevier, *AI: The Tumultuous Search for Artificial Intelligence* (New York: BasicBooks, 1993), 96.
13. AI researcher Thomas Binford is said to have kept a sign over his desk at MIT that read 'We shall overclaim'. Thomas Binford, 'The Machine Sees', in *Robotics*, edited by Marvin Minsky (New York: Doubleday, 1985), 99.

The incredible operational speed of Deep Blue, which was said to be able to examine 200 million moves per second, was a result of the rapid hardware innovations from the 1950 through the 1990s, innovations that increased computing power exponentially, with the number of transistors in an integrated circuit roughly doubling every two years, an increase known as Moore's Law. A reliance on the continuation of exponential growth in computing power promised by Moore's Law is one factor in the recent upsurge in predictions that an AGI is once again right around the corner.

In his 2006 book, *The Singularity is Near*, futurist Ray Kurzweil believes that this exponential growth in computing power will lead us, not only to an AGI by 2045, but also

> to transcend the limitations of our bodies and brains. We will gain power over our fates. Our mortality will be in our own hands . . . We will fully understand human thinking and will be able to vastly extend and expand its reach. By the end of this century the nonbiological portion of our intelligence will be trillions of trillions of times more powerful than unaided human intelligence.[14]

Gordon Moore, after whom the law is named, disagrees: '[Moore's Law] can't continue forever. The nature of exponentials is that you push them out and eventually disaster happens.'[15] So far our increases in computational power have been largely due to miniaturisation. Moore believes that as our circuits approach the size of atoms, we will reach a limit, thus halting or significantly slowing computational increase. Microsoft guru and internet pioneer Jaron Lanier raises a different objection, noting that Moore's Law only applies to hardware innovation, not software:

> If anything, there's a reverse Moore's Law observable in software: As processors become faster and memory becomes cheaper, software becomes correspondingly slower and more bloated, using up all available resources . . . We have better

---

14. Raymond Kurzweil, *The Singularity is Near: When Humans Transcend Biology* (New York: Penguin, 2006), 9.
15. Manek Dubash, 'Moore's Law is dead, says Gordon Moore', in *Techworld*, April 13, 2010. https://www.techworld.com/news/tech-innovation/moores-law-is-dead-says-gordon-moore-3576581/ Retrieved 8/6/18.

speech recognition and language translation than we used to, for example, and we are learning to run larger data bases and networks. But our core techniques and technologies for software simply haven't kept up with hardware.[16]

Proponents of a Singularity such as Musk or Kurzweil point to recent gains in AI technology propelled by 'deep learning', a technique that uses multiple processing layers and a supervised trial and error method combined with statistical analyses to discover patterns in large data sets. This technique has spawned major advances in speech and visual recognition, object detection, and in scientific areas such as genomics and particle acceleration.[17] Unlike usual symbolic programming, programmers of deep learning applications do not explicitly tell the computer what to do and, thus, do not always know how the program reaches the conclusions it does. Another technique, 'reinforcement learning', allows the computer to practice a skill while unsupervised, simply knowing the desired outcome. The AlphaGo program that beat South Korean Go master Lee Sedol in 2016 used this technique. As promising as they are, these techniques do not amount to an AGI. AlphaGo does not know it is playing a game, nor can it generate general principles. And it is, of course, still a weak AI in the sense that it only plays games.

This has led many in the field to the conclusion that to construct a true AGI we would have to reverse engineer the human brain. Several projects, including MIT's Mind Machine Project, the US BRAIN Initiative, and the European Union's Human Brain Project seek to map the connectome of the brain in much the same way as the Human Genome Project successfully mapped our DNA. While the Human Genome project was a large and ambitious undertaking, reverse engineering the human brain is vastly more difficult. It is estimated that the brain contains roughly 80-90 billion neurons, each of which can potentially be connected to thousands of other neurons.

These connections are not permanent, but continually changing as we experience new things, forget others, age, or have a beer or two. And the connectome would not be, in and of itself, sufficient. Electrical impulses move from neuron to neuron enhanced or impeded by

---

16. Jaron Lanier, 'One Half a Manifesto', in *Wired* 1 December, 2000,
17. Yann LeCun, Yoshua Bengio, & Geoffrey Hinton. 'Deep Learning', in *Nature* 521/28 (May, 2015): 436–444.

a continuous bath of chemical neurotransmitters, such as dopamine or serotonin. These transmitters play a huge role in the workings of our brain, as evidenced by those with diseases such as Parkinson's in which these transmitters are diminished. We are also only now learning about the role our guts play, not only through the network of more than 100 million neurons in our digestive system, but through the microbiota that lives there. We have long known that the brain has a direct effect on the stomach. We now know the converse is true. The stomach can have a direct effect on the brain. An impaired microbiota can cause anxiety, stress, and even clinical depression.[18] Likewise, a healthy gut can lift one's mood and plays an integral role in our sense of well-being.

One might argue that our gut cannot compose a sonata or solve a mathematical equation. It plays a part in our emotional life, but, like Mr Spock in Star Trek, we could do without all those messy emotions. But could we? Obviously, a life without emotion is not a fully human life. More than that, our emotions play a large role in volition. Persons who have brain damage in the regions of the brain that govern emotion lose much of their decision-making ability.[19] How do I know what to get for lunch if I do not want anything? Emotions give us the drive to do things. One aspect of clinical depression is the loss of interest in things that normally give us pleasure, a tendency to procrastinate, and the inability to carry through with plans.

Even if we overcame the complexity issues above, would a reproduction of a human brain be operable? Juan Enriquez, Managing Director of Excel Venture Management, writes: 'But if it turned out that all data erases upon transplant, that knowledge is unique to the individual organism, (in other words that there is something innate and individual to consciousness-knowledge-intelligence), then simply copying the dazzlingly complex connectome of brains into machines would likely not lead to an operative intelligence.'[20] Here we have the hard question of consciousness. Certain feature of con-

18. 'The Gut-Brain Connection', Harvard Health, https://www.health.harvard.edu/diseases-and-conditions/the-gut-brain-connection, Accessed 7/21/2018.
19. Antoine Bechara, Hanna Damasio, and Antonio R Damasio, 'Emotion, Decision Making and the Orbitofrontal Cortex', in *Cerebral Cortex*, 10/3 (1 March 2000): 295–307.
20. Juan Enriquez, 'Head Transplants?' http://edge.org/response-detail/26058. Accessed 8/9 2018.

sciousness, such as a sense of self or of having free will, depend on particular structures of the brain. What we do not know is how or even whether these parts of the brain generate these aspects of consciousness.

Therefore, while I expect we will learn a great deal about the functionality of our brains from these projects, there are gaps between that understanding and a functional AGI. It seems to me quite unlikely that we will have a computer that can outthink us any time in the near future, if ever. MIT's Rodney Brooks agrees:

> In my view, having ideas is easy. Turning them into reality is hard. Turning them into being deployed at scale is even harder. Building human level intelligence and human level physical capability is really, really hard. There has been a little tiny burst of progress over the last five years, and too many people think it is all done. In reality we are less than 1% of the way there, with no real intellectual ideas yet on how to get to 5%.[21]

The Real Threats

While fears of a super-intelligent robot apocalypse may be premature, that does not mean AI gives us nothing to worry about right now. Even 'weak' AI has already begun to upend our economy, our politics, and even our sex lives. And this is only the beginning. Despite its currently posing little threat to 'the human race', as Hawking fears, AI does pose several threats to the structure of human civilization as we know it.

First, consider the economy. A study from the National Bureau of Economic Research estimates that automation has eliminated hundreds of thousands of jobs in the US since the 1990s. For every three jobs lost only one new job in the computer industry is created.[22] It is automation, far more than governmental regulations or off shoring, that has decimated industrial sector employment. No matter what President Trump says, jobs in coal or manufacturing are not coming

---

21. Rodney Brooks, 'My Dated Predictions', https://rodneybrooks.com/my-dated-predictions/. Accessed 8/9/2018.
22. Daron Acemoglu and Pascual Restrepo, 'Robots and Jobs: Evidence from US Labor Markets', National Bureau of Economic Research Working Paper No. 23285, March 2017, http://www.nber.org/papers/w23285. Accessed 8/9/18.

back. Moreover, automated vehicles and Amazon are poised to take over transportation and retail.

Nor are blue-collar workers the only ones who should worry. A 2013 University of Oxford report estimated that 47 percent of American jobs will be threatened by automation in the coming decades, including many white-collar jobs in the legal, health, and educational sectors.[23] The World Bank estimates that this proportion is even higher in developing countries.[24] AI has begun to shake the foundation of Western capitalism.

Second, this has obvious ramifications for our political systems, and we have seen the first of these in the election of Donald Trump in the US and the vote for Brexit in the UK. Beyond the restiveness of the working class, AI also played a role in our last election through the spread of fake news on social media by bots. Artificial intelligence makes the development of fake evidence remarkably easy. A recent study published in the journal *Cognitive Research: Principles and Implications* found that people could not identify whether or not a photo had been Photoshopped with any more accuracy than guessing: 'Photos are incredibly powerful. They influence how we see the world. They can even influence our memory of things. If we can't tell the fake ones from the real ones, the fakes are going to be powerful, too.'[25]

It is not only Photoshop. A recent article in *Wired*, entitled 'AI Will Make Forging Anything Entirely Too Easy', notes that video and audio are subject to similar falsification. 'In the future, realistic-looking and -sounding fakes will constantly confront people. Awash in audio, video, images, and documents, many real but some fake,

---

23. Carl Frey and Michael Osborne, 'The Future of Employment: How Susceptible are Jobs to Computerisation?' 9/17/17, https://www.oxfordmartin.ox.ac.uk/downloads/academic/The_Future_of_Employment.pdf. Accessed 8/9/18.
24. See 'Are You Afraid of Losing Your Job to Automation?' https://www.worldbank.org/en/news/feature/2017/07/11/robotizacion-mercado-trabajo. Accessed 8/9/18.
25. Sophie Nightingale, Kimberley Wade, and Derrick Watson, 'Can people identify original and manipulated photos of real-world scenes?', in *Cognitive Research: Principles and* Implications, 20172:30, 18 July 2017, https://cognitiveresearchjournal.springeropen.com/articles/10.1186/s41235-017-0067-2. Accessed 8/9/18.

people will struggle to know whom and what to trust.'[26] This has led to a new form of espionage, one the Russians pioneered in our last election. While in the past, espionage was about obtaining information, in the future it will also be about inserting information wherever one can. AI has begun to shake the foundation of our trust in our media and our political campaigns.

Third, our private lives stand to be altered as well. According to a 2016 study from the University of Duisenberg-Essen fifty per cent of men surveyed said they could imagine purchasing a sex robot within the next five years.[27] Sex robots are already selling well, particularly in Japan, where their use has already led to a decline in human-human sexual encounters. Here is one threat to humanity that might truly fall under the rubric of "existential."

Dreams of Power and the Sleep of Reason

In the Walt Disney movie Fantasia, there is an episode entitled 'The Sorcerer's Apprentice'. Mickey, left with the task of filling the workshop water tank, pages through a book of magic and casts a spell on a broom, giving it the task of toting the water from well to tank. Relieved of his chore, Mickey goes to sleep dreaming of power and glory, while the broom dutifully brings in bucket after bucket of water. The broom, having but one instruction, brings in more and more water, flooding the workshop and waking a hapless Mickey, who does not know how to stop it from its single-minded devotion to its task.

AI might bring a similarly tragic result. Computers lead us to treat people as data, overwhelm us with too much information, separate us by catering to our preferences, and provide an all too tempting diversion. In a recent article in *The Atlantic*, Henry Kissinger warns that '[t]he digital world's emphasis on speed inhibits reflection; its incentive empowers the radical over the thoughtful; its values are

---

26. Greg Allen, 'AI Will Make Forging Anything Entirely Too Easy', in *Wired* 1 July 2017. https://www.wired.com/story/ai-will-make-forging-anything-entirely-too-easy/. Accessed 8/9/18.
27. Astrid Marieke Rosenthal-von der Pütten, 'Experimental Investigation of the Uncanny Valley Phenomenon', unpublished doctoral dissertation. https://duepublico.uni-duisburg-essen.de/servlets/DerivateServlet/Derivate-34866/Rosenthal-v.d.P_Diss.pdf. Accessed 8/9/18.

shaped by subgroup consensus, not by introspection.'[28] After nodding to the possibilities for 'extraordinary benefits' in medical science (AI is already better at detecting cancer than many clinicians),[29] clean-energy provision, and other environmental issues, Kissinger warns of AI's potential for unintended consequences, especially those that may arise from the inability of an AI to contextualise. Like Mickey's broom, which was told nothing about the size of the water tank or the undesirability of a flooded workshop, AI may not be able to 'comprehend the context that informs its instructions'. Kissinger asks, 'Can we, at an early stage, detect and correct an AI program that is acting outside our framework of expectation? Or will AI, left to its own devices, inevitably develop slight deviations that could, over time, cascade into catastrophic departures?'[30] The latter is, perhaps, what should worry us most. As Sir Nigel Shadbolt, professor of computer science at Oxford, recently noted, 'The danger is clearly not that robots will decide to put us away and have a robot revolution . . . If there [are] killer robots, it will be because we've been stupid enough to give it the instructions or software for it to do that without having a human in the loop deciding.'[31]

Recall the game-playing program AlphaGo, programmed only to win. I fear that, just as Go can be reduced to 'winning', so, too, in other areas, the single-mindedness of AI, like the single-mindedness of Mickey's broom, might narrow the way we think of our tasks and our world. Mickey never thought about the exercise he was losing or the joy he might have found in going out to the well and looking at the sky.

There is a classic story from the early days of machine learning is of a program devised by the Department of Defence that was given the task of learning to locate hidden tanks. The machine got quite

28. Henry Kissinger, 'How the Enlightenment Ends', in *The Atlantic*, June 2018. https://www.theatlantic.com/magazine/archive/2018/06/henry-kissinger-ai-could-mean-the-end-of-human-history/559124/. Accessed 8/9/18.

29. 'AI in Cancer Detection and Diagnosis', in *Springer Nature*, 23 May 2018, https://grandchallenges.springernature.com/users/70416-nature-research/posts/33492-ai-in-cancer-detection-and-diagnosis. Accessed 8/9/18.

30. Kissinger.

31. Hannah Devlin, 'Killer robots will only exist if we are stupid enough to let them', in *The Guardian*, 11 June 2018, https://www.theguardian.com/technology/2018/jun/11/killer-robots-will-only-exist-if-we-are-stupid-enough-to-let-them. Accessed 8/9/18.

proficient at identifying all the pictures with tanks in its initial set, but when given a new set of pictures, totally failed. It turned out that the photos in the training set harbouring hidden tanks were all taken on cloudy days. The machine had learned nothing about tanks but knew how to distinguish a cloudy from a sunny day.

Whether true or apocryphal, this story illustrates how machine learning programs may reach conclusions that we do not understand. Kissinger notes, '[AI] algorithms, being mathematical interpretations of observed data, do not explain the underlying reality that produces them. Paradoxically, as the world becomes more transparent, it will also become increasingly mysterious.'[32]

AI is likely to be as inscrutable as the spells in the sorcerer's magic book. We will know it works, but we won't know how—thus we may find it as hard to control as Mickey's industrious broom. The broom had no intention of causing trouble. It did what it was told. AI will do the same. The problem is that we, like Mickey, are filled with dreams of power and glory while being mere beginners in casting our spells over our mechanical servants.

In his Gifford lectures, *The Nature and Destiny of Man*, Reinhold Niebuhr noted that dreams of power are a part of the human condition. We are the one creature with the mental ability to transcend both the mind itself, through self-contemplation, and the natural world, through technology. However, Niebuhr is adamant that this transcendence does not obviate our physical nature and its limitations. Niebuhr writes:

> Man is ignorant and involved in the limitations of the finite mind, but he pretends that he is not limited. He assumes that he can gradually transcend finite limitations until his mind becomes identical with universal mind. All of his intellectual and cultural pursuits, therefore, become infected with the sin of pride.[33]

We pretend to an 'ignorance of our ignorance'. Niebuhr sees this ignorance as perhaps the greatest flaw in modern scientific thought, which asserts 'that its philosophy is a final philosophy because it rests

---

32. Kissinger.
33. Reinhold Niebuhr, *The Nature and Destiny of Man, Volume 1: Human Nature* (New York: Scribner's, 1941), 178–79.

upon science, a certainty which betrays ignorance of its own prejudices and failure to recognize the limits of scientific knowledge'.[34] He goes on to say:

> Man stands at the juncture of nature and spirit; and is involved in both freedom and necessity. His sin is never the mere ignorance of his ignorance. It is always partly an effort to obscure his blindness by overestimating the degree of his sight and to obscure his insecurity by stretching his power beyond its limits.[35]

Computer scientist Joseph Weitzenbaum agrees. He writes:

> The rhetoric of the technological intelligentsia may be attractive because it appears to be an invitation to reason. It is that, indeed. But, as I have argued, it urges instrumental reasonings, not authentic human rationality. It advertises easy and 'scientifically' endorsed answers to all conceivable problems. It exploits the myth of expertise.[36]

AI currently exploits the myth that we understand ourselves, our minds, and our world. Mickey thought he understood water carrying spells. He didn't. Nor do we understand the spells we cast when we unloose what we think of as 'intelligent' programs.

So, what are we to do? First, we must avoid the category error of personifying AI. A computer program cannot be, in Martin Buber's terms, a Thou. It is always an It. It has no consciousness, no emotions, no will of its own and these things are not 'right around the corner'. The idea, often espoused by computer scientists such as Kurzweil or Bostrom, that just a little more complexity will suddenly cause consciousness to emerge is, in my opinion, risible. We are still a long way from knowing what consciousness is nor where it comes from.

In the meantime, we would do well to think of AI, then, as a means rather than an end. Like all technologies, AI is a tool. As such, it is not just a means of power over nature, but primarily a means of power by some persons over other persons and thus a source of

34. Niebuhr, *The Nature and Destiny of Man, Volume 1: Human*, 195.
35. Niebuhr, *The Nature and Destiny of Man, Volume 1: Human*, 181.
36. Joseph Weitzenbaum, *Computer Power and Human Reason: From Judgment to Calculation* (New York: WH Freeman, 1976), 253.

injustice. Niebuhr notes that our technologies not only disrupt the natural world but also the social world: 'The ego which falsely makes itself the centre of existence in its pride and will-to-power inevitably subordinates other life to its will and thus does injustice.'[37] Thus, the fundamental questions we must ask remain the same: How do I love God and neighbor with all my heart, all my soul, and all my minds? And who is my neighbor?

Artificial Intelligence will disrupt our lives. Mindless programs will overtake many of our currently mindless jobs. Data mining will give us new correlations on which we will base an increasing number of decisions, some of them leading to false premises and unjust actions. Social media and robotic sex partners will take the place of authentic face to face relationships. We do not need a Singularity nor super-intelligence for AI to change the ways we interact with one another and structure out society. And AI will not tell us how to respond to these changes. Only we have the freedom to decide, day to day, when to rely on our computers and when not. We must not abdicate that freedom, preferring, as Mickey did, dreams of power to the hard work of reality.

---

37. Niebuhr, 179.

Artificial Intelligence,
Transhumanism, and Frankenfear

Ted Peters

'The will to mastery becomes all the more urgent the more technology threatens to slip from human control.'
– Martin Heidegger[1]

Abstract. Even if AI (artificial intelligence) at a level beyond rapid computation, machine learning, and cute gadgets never comes to pass, theologians must speculate along with transhumanist visionaries about the prospect of superintelligence, the prophesied extinction of *Homo sapiens,* and the survival of a posthuman species. While advances in AI technology that benefit humanity should be celebrated, extravagant utopian promises should be met with a healthy dose of Frankenfear, that is, caution.

Key Terms. Artificial Intelligence, Intelligence Amplification, robot, robotcalypse, globotics, transhumanism, H+, posthuman, anxiety, *imago Dei,* theology, Tower of Babel, Prometheus, Frankenstein

Bio. Ted Peters teaches systematic theology and ethics at the Graduate Theological Union in Berkeley, California, USA. He co-edits the journal, *Theology and Science,* at the Center for Theology and the Natural Sciences. He is author of *God--The World's Future* (Fortress, 3rd ed, 2015) and co-author of *Evolution from Creation to New Creation* (Abingdon 2002). Along with two colleagues he is editing a new book, *Religious Transhumanism and its Crit-*

---

1. Martin Heidegger, *The Question Concerning Technology and Other Essays* [*Die Frage nach der Technik* 1949], translated by William Lovitt in *Basic Writings,* edited by J Glen Gray and John Stambaugh (New York: Harper, 1977) 5. *Philosophical Posthumanism*, in contrast to Transhumanism, 'follows on Heidegger's reflection that technology cannot be reduced to mere means, nor to a reification, and thus cannot be mastered'. Francesca Ferrando, *Philosophical Posthumanism* (Heidelberg: Springer, 2019) 42.

ics (Lexington). He is author of a fiction thriller with a Transhumanist plot, *Cyrus Twelve,* with Aprocryphile Press. Visit his website: TedsTimelyTake. com.

In the climax of Dan Brown's best-selling thriller, *Origin,* antagonist Edmond Kirsch espouses a galvanic transhumanist philosophy. He announces triumphantly that the era of religion is past and that the future belongs to science. 'I believe we are on the brink of an enlightened new era, a world where religion finally departs...and science reigns'.[2] Science will deliver a material transformation that our religious ancestors could only envision spiritually. 'Humans are evolving into something different . . . We are becoming a hybrid species—a fusion of biology and technology'.[3] This hybrid species will create a utopian future, a future in which 'breakthrough technologies' will create such an abundance of humankind's critical resources that warring over them would no longer be necessary'.[4] Breakthrough technologies will lead to the end of war, to utopia. The era of religion is over now, because science has become our savior.

But, can we rightly call it 'salvation'? Not according to Bill Joy, founder of Sun Microsystems, who in 2000 pessimistically forecasted the extinction of the human race.

> As society and the problems that face it become more and more complex and machines become more and more intelligent, people will let machines make more of their decisions for them, simply because machine-made decisions will bring better results than man-made ones. Eventually a stage may be reached at which the decisions necessary to keep the system running will be so complex that human beings will be incapable of making them intelligently. At that stage the machines will be in effective control. People won't be able to just turn the machines off, because they will be so dependent on them that turning them off would amount to suicide.[5]

---

2.   Dan Brown, *Origin* (New York: Bantam Press, 2017), 291.
3.   Brown, *Origin,* 411.
4.   Brown, *Origin,* 412.
5.   Bill Joy, 'Why the Future Doesn't Need Us', in *Wired* (April 2000); https://www. wired.com/2000/04/joy-2/ (accessed 11/28/2016).

Shortly after crossing this AI threshold, the human species will die off and be replaced by the post-human, by superintelligence.

How should soon-to-be-obsolete theologians think about this? This is the question computer scientist and Quaker theologian Noreen Herzfeld asks: 'Do our technologies threaten religion itself? We used to believe in the power of God. Have we replaced that belief with a belief in the power of our own technologies?'[6] Roman Catholic theologian Brian Patrick Green answers with a call to action. 'Scholars of religion and theologians should seriously engage technology because it is empowering humanity in ways that were previously reserved only for gods.'[7]

Here's the challenge: through technological self-transformation, *Homo sapiens* are about to summit the Tower of Babel. On the one hand, according to the Dan Brown scenario, we will find apotheosis atop the Tower of Babel; the successors to *Homo sapiens* will have become *Homo deus*. On the other hand, according to the Bill Joy scenario, the attempt to summit the Tower of Babel will end in tragedy, with the extinction of *Homo sapiens*. Worse. It will have been a self-inflicted self-extinction. Instead of utopia, we will have achieved oblivion.

Does AI (artificial intelligence) in computers or robots augmented by IA (intelligence amplification through deep brain implants) place our cyborg generation at a crossroads?[8] Is it utopia versus oblivion? Or, more specifically, will the pursuit of utopia inadvertently lead to oblivion? Can we anticipate a tragedy in the making? Does anybody

---

6. Noreen Herzfeld, 'Introduction: Religion and the New Technologies', in *Religions* 8:7 (2017): 1–3, at 2; file:///C:/Users/Ted/Downloads/religions-08-00129-v2%20(2).pdf.

7. Brian Patrick Green, 'The Catholic Church and Technological Progress: Past, Present, and Future', in *Religions* 8:6 (2017): 2–16, at 1; file:///C:/Users/Ted/Downloads/religions-08-00106-v2.pdf.

8. 'Often cyborgs and other posthuman hybrids are seen as figures of the monstrous, moral abominations resulting from the transgression of ontological boundaries. Just as a common ancestry with nonhuman animals seems to threaten the ontological distinctiveness of humanity, so too can the technological innovation of the cyborg, as it presumes an ontological kinship with the nonhuman machine.' Anne Kull, 'Cyborg or Religious? Technonature and Technoculture', in *Science et Fides* 4:1 (January 2016): 295–311, at 302; http://apcz.umk.pl/czasopisma/index.php/SetF/article/view/SetF.2016.016/8762.

remember the warnings of the Tower of Babel? Prometheus? Frankenstein?

The Immediate Frankenfear: The Robotcalypse

Anxiety over the long-term future of the human race has not set in
yet. Where we find anxiety is in the fear that tomorrow's AI will eliminate today's jobs. Californians fear the coming of the *robotcalypse*, the
loss of eight hundred million jobs to robots by the year 2030.[9] Not
only Californians! Globalization combined with aggressive robotics
has provoked a Frankenfear of an imminent 'Globotics Upheaval'.[10]

But, only some of us dread the loss. Others foresee opportunity,
especially in Australia. 'The number of jobs in the merging industry
around artificial intelligence (AI), including work on self-driving cars
and smart digital assistants, is growing in Australia but so is interest
from job seekers . . . the number of AI-related job posts has doubled
since 2015 and, at the same time, search activity by job seekers has
tripled.'[11] Optimists believe that new high-tech jobs will more than
replace those lost. 'This job growth (jobs gained) could more than

---

9. Tad Friend, 'Golden Boy 2.0: Gavin Newsom's Life in California Politics', in *New
    Yorker* (November 5, 2018): 18–26, at 22. 'For people who give purpose to their
    lives through their work, this loss will be very serious indeed. But many, if not
    most, people do not get their life's meaning from their work. Instead they get
    it from their family, their religion, their community, their hobbies, their sports
    teams, or other sources, and so life for many people may go on. However, all of
    this assumes that the unemployed will somehow be fed and sheltered, despite
    their lack of gainful employment; and this assumption might not be correct,
    particularly in nations with weak social safety nets. Inequality will almost
    certainly increase, as those who are masters of AI labor gather that slice of wealth
    that once would have gone to paying for human labor.' Brian Patrick Green,
    'Ethical Reflections on Artificial Intelligence', in *Science et Fides* 6:2 (2018): 1–23,
    at 12.
10. Richard Baldwin, *The Globotics Upheaval: Globalization, Robotics, and the Future
    of Work* (Oxford UK: Oxford University Press, 2019).
11. Chris Pash, 'The emerging jobs being created in artificial intelligence in Australia',
    in *Business Insider* (March 12, 2018) https://www.businessinsider.com.au/
    the-emerging-jobs-being-created-in-artificial-intelligence-in-australia-2018-3
    (accessed 10/2/2018).

offset the jobs lost to automation'.[12] Does this mean our anxiety will be alleviated?

Worry over AI is not ubiquitous. Creative new applications of AI are bursting upon us like pop corn. Computerized art work seems to elicit no anxiety. The first two exhibitions of computer generated paintings took place in Germany in 1965. The Institute of Contemporary Arts in London held a show, 'Cybernetic Serendipity', in 1968. In 2018, Christies auctioned off its first portrait generated by an AI algorithm. After a half century, digital art has added only a slow lane to the fine arts traffic. Rather than worry about competition, ol' fashioned artists mixing their oils register at most an 'oh, hum'.

In Spain the police rely on AI to distinguish between fake and real claims of robbery. The police fed their computer, VeriPol, data from 1,112 robbery cases, some fake and some genuine. After deep learning, VeriPol outperformed cops by nearly twenty percent in tagging those cheaters who fake a robbery to collect insurance.[13]

In Sweden thousands of customers are buying smart chips the size of a rice grain with 2KB memory to be surgically inserted into their hands near the thumb. In the brain such a chip would provide intelligence amplification (IA), but in the thumb it electronically transfers information to share LinkedIn identification, to permit buying tickets to take the train, to pay for restaurant meals, and such. Some hold 'chipping parties' for the insertion ritual. Again, no anxiety here.[14]

The promise of AI robotics is actually ambiguous. There is a chance that good things might include risk. On December 5, 2018, a robot accidently punctured a container of bear repellent in the New Jersey warehouse of Amazon. In this instance, a dozen employees were exposed and hospitalized, one critically. Amazon robots have a

12. Dom Galeon, 'McKinsey Finds Automation Could Eradicate a Third of America's Jobs by 2030', in *Futurism* November 30, 2017, https://futurism.com/mckinsey-finds-automation-eradicate-third-americas-workforce-2030.
13. Emiliano Rodriguez Mega, 'Lie-Detector AI', in *Scientific American* 320:2 (February 2019): 14.
14. Maddy Savage, 'Thousands of Swedes are Inserting Microchips Under Their Skin', National Public Radio (October 22, 2018) https://www.npr.org/2018/10/22/658808705/thousands-of-swedes-are-inserting-microchips-under-their-skin?utm_source=facebook.com&utm_medium=social&utm_campaign=npr&utm_term=nprnews&utm_content=2050&t=1540283166307 (accessed 23/10/2018).

history of making costly mistakes.[15] We need not worry that robots will set the bar of perfection too high.

From robots making a mess to robots cleaning up a mess we now turn. To clean up the radioactive mess left by the 2011 tsunami and nuclear meltdown at Japan's Fukushima power plant, mopper-uppers have sent in remotely-controlled robots, because radiation levels are too high for humans. Unfortunately, however, the androids have failed. They have been overpowered by radiation. This leaves Tokyo Electric Power Company (TEPCO) with a major decommissioning struggle on its hands.

Will the advance of AI exacerbate the rift between rich and poor? Melanie Smallman at London's Turing Institute fears that it will. The UK government just rolled out its *code of conduct for artificial intelligence (AI) systems used by NHS.*[16] Smallman complains: this is inadequate to regulate AI! Why? Because it underestimates the social upheaval that will follow. It fails to make a systems analysis which would reveal that AI innovations in medicine will widen 'inequality' as 'an unintended side effect'. The problem 'is embedded in the technologies themselves . . . investment in surgical robots draws funds from other treatments and centralises care in large teaching hospitals, requiring many patients to travel longer distances or forego care'. A leap forward in AI means a leap backward in social equality. 'The UK code is a missed opportunity to start things off right, to anticipate wider, inevitable problems and to keep the healthy system affordable and effective.'[17] In short, technological triumphs are morally ambiguous.

---

15. Luis Matsakis, 'This wasn't even Amazon's first repellant accident', in *Wired* (12/6/2018);   https://www.wired.com/story/amazon-first-bear-repellent-accident/.

16. Department of Health and Social Care UK, *New code of conduct for artificial intelligence (AI) systems used by NHS;* https://www.gov.uk/government/news/new-code-of-conduct-for-artificial-intelligence-ai-systems-used-by-the-nhs (accessed 2019). Deep Mind, founded independently in 2010 and acquired by Google in 2014, is adding a department of ethics and society; https://deepmind.com/about/.

17. Melanie Smallman, 'Policies designed for drugs won't work for AI', in *Nature* 567:7746 (7 March 2019): 7.

Should Sexbots Have Rights?

Here is an additional question: should robots have rights? More specifically, does the 'Me Too' movement require that we humans treat sexbots as persons with rights? Why might we ask such a question? Because one planner of a sex robot brothel requires that his customers seek consent from the robot before commencing with sex. 'Don't forget to ask your sex robot for consent', says Unicole Unicron.[18] Unicron's plan is to rent out life-sized Barbie style sex robots by the hour to customers who want to make love to AI with a vagina and other orifices. But only as long as the robot agrees to it. Yes, the sexbot will come equipped with a chat box to carry on a kinky sex conversation. But, we must still ask: is anybody home in such a robot? Is there a self? An agent? A person? If not, then might consent be superfluous? This controversy stirs up little more than a few smiles.

In short, the accomplishments, failures, and threats of AI have to date elicited at best an overreaching anticipation and at worst an "oh hum" response within the consuming public. Change and even progress are so expected that advances in AI are not likely to shock anyone. Producers of AI products tout only the utopian benefits their future will bring. The Inception Institute of Artificial Intelligence (IIAI), for example, places AI 'at the heart of a happier, healthier, and more productive global community'.[19] Such promises calm anxiety and excite enthusiasm, even if they are doubtful.

---

18. Cited by Emily Shurgerman, 'California Cult Leader Unicole Unicron Plans Sex Robot Brothel--With a Twist', *Daily Beast* (11/24/2018); https://www.thedailybeast.com/california-cult-leader-uniclone-unicron-plans-sex-robot-brothelwith-a-twist?via=newsletter&source=Weekend. Real Doll already sells sexbots. https://www.yourdoll.com/160cm-sex-doll-golp-3/?gclid=Cj0KCQiArenfBRCoARIsAFc1FqfvOqLV_P6O43zZlNgX2LStEGQt1WIsgyUJCG9yvHvDyPysL3RnbsEaAh2xEALw_wcB.
19. 'Inception Institute of Artificial Intelligence: A Bold Initiative to Foster Global AI Research and Innovation', in *Science* 361:6408 (21 September 2018): 1168–1169. One issue being addressed is the doctrine of *technological manifest destiny*, according to which the purveyors of new technology shun responsibility for social impact. 'The polite term for the delusions that grip the lords of Silicon Valley (and their fans elsewhere) is *technological determinism*: the belief that technology is what really drives history and that they are on the right side of that history. It may also explain why they have manifested such blithe indifference to the malign effects that their machines are having on society. After all, if technology is the remorseless bulldozer that flattens everything in its path,

It is difficult to know if we are underestimating or overestimating the impact of new technologies. What we can perceive is tension. The underlying tension is the apparent misfit between human meaning, on the one hand, and the impersonal nature of science and technology, on the other. Philosopher Daniel Dennett brings this source of anxiety to articulation.

> When we start treating living bodies as motherboards in which to assemble cyborgs, or as spare parts collections to be sold to the highest bidder, where will it all end? . . .,We are entering a new conceptual world, thanks to science, and it does not harmonize comfortably with our traditional conceptions of our lives and what they mean.[20]

With this tension in mind, the task of the public theologian becomes one of mapping the road to meaning at the intersection of humanity and technology.

Can We Rely on AI to be Moral?

Will artificial intelligence be morally neutral? Or, morally responsible? If the latter, which moral code will our favorite robots live by?

Isaac Azimov introduced us to robot morality to make science fiction reading exciting. Recall the internal logic of the three laws.

1. A robot may not injure a human being or, through inaction, allow a human being to come to harm.
2. A robot must obey the orders given it by human beings except where such orders would conflict with the First Law.

---

then why waste time and energy fretting about it or imagining that it might be controlled? Determinism, in that sense, removes human agency from the picture. The role assigned to people is essentially that of passive or active consumers of whatever wonders the tech industry chooses to lay before them.' John Naughton, 'Think the giants of Silicon Valley have your best interests at heart? Think again', in *The Guardian* (October 21, 2018) US Edition, italics added; https://www.theguardian.com/commentisfree/2018/oct/21/think-the-giants-of-silicon-valley-have-your-best-interestsat-heart-think-again?CMP=share_btn_link.

20. Daniel C Dennett, 'How to Protect Human Dignity from Science', in *Human Dignity and Bioethics,* ed, U.S. President's Council on Bioethics (Washington DC: www.bioethics.gov, 2008) 39-59, at 41; https://www.academia.edu/38307610/Human_dignity_and_bioethics?email_work_card=thumbnail-desktop.

3. A robot must protect its own existence as long as such protection does not conflict with the First or Second Laws.[21]

Despite the use of these rules as a literary device, the logic illuminates our intuitive need to protect both human life and robotic existence. In a moral dilemma, protection of human life takes moral precedence. These rules seem clearer than Sinai's Ten Commandments.

But, how do we communicate this to the robot? As of this writing, no robots are sufficiently intelligent or autonomous to render independent moral judgments. This means that the first stage of AI moral development will have to be pre-programmed algorithmically according to human morality. But, whose human morality?

How will AI programmers know what to dictate to the robot's decision tree? The Ten Commandments? Buddhism's Eightfold Path? The Scout Law? How will a robot handle differences in moral opinion let alone moral dilemmas?

A recent survey discovered such a range of public opinion regarding moral priorities that makes it impossible to formulate a single universal moral code. Survey respondents could not agree, for example, on what self-driving vehicles should do to avoid collisions or killing pedestrians. The researchers 'found that people from countries with strong government institutions, such as Finland and Japan, more often chose to hit people who were crossing the road illegally than did respondents in nations with weaker institutions, such as Nigeria or Pakistan.'[22] What!? And, the survey revealed that Europeans are more willing to sacrifice the lives of older pedestrians on behalf of younger people whereas, in contrast, East Asians are more protective of their seniors. Moral priorities apparently differ.

When self-driving cars finally fill the roads of Europe, should senior citizens migrate to China where Confucian respect for elders is still intact? Or, should seniors arm their canes, crutches, and wheel chairs with defensive electronics? Could we ask a Chinese AI engineer to invent an electronic wand that shuts off the engine and applies the brakes of a self-driving car just before impact? And sell it

---

21. Isaac Azimov, *I, Robot* (1950).
22. Amy Maxmen, 'Self-Driving car dilemmas reveal that moral choices are not universal', in *Nature* (24 October 2018) https://www.nature.com/articles/d41586-018-07135-0.

in Europe? But, then, who will program the wand? Is there a reason for Frankenfear here?

A healthy dose of Frankenfear might be realistic, at least according to Brian Patrick Green. 'Just as human intelligence is a powerful force, so too will AI be. Just as humans can apply their intelligence towards evil ends, finding ever newer and more fiendish ways to harm each other, so too will AI, at the bidding of its human masters.'[23] In short, what we should rightly fear is ourselves. The activity of robots will mime human sinfulness.

Where does this leave us? It means our ethicists will have to work overtime before autonomous machines such as self-driving vehicles jam our highways.

> Even if ethicists were to agree on how autonomous vehicles should solve moral dilemmas, their work would be useless if citizens were to disagree with their solution and thus opt out of the future that autonomous vehicles promise in lieu of the status quo. Any attempt to devise artificial intelligence ethics must be at least cognizant of public morality.[24]

Now, note what this debate presupposes. It presupposes that autonomous robots will not be intelligent in the full sense of having a self that deliberates, decides, and acts according to its own commitment to a moral code. That moral code will be decided in advance by an ethical engineer at the assembly plant. Retrodictively, what does this imply about the present level of artificial intelligence?

Is Artificial Intelligence Really Intelligent?

Artificial intelligence isn't. Computers make superb calculators, to be sure.[25] But, intelligent they are not. Will machines ever be intelligent?

---

23. Brian Patrick Green, 'Ethical Reflections on Artificial Intelligence', in *Science et Fides* 6:2 (2018): 1–23, at 8.

24. Edmund Awad, Sohan Dsousa, Richard Kim, Jonathan Schulz, Joseph Henrich, Azim Shariff, Jean-Francois Bonnefon, Lyad Rahman, 'The Moral Machine experiment', in *Nature* (24 October 2018) https://www.nature.com/articles/s41586-018-0637-6.

25. Machine learning amazes us, to be sure. Yet, the algorithmic analysis process requires further development before machine learning can be trusted. 'Machine-learning tools can also turn up fool's gold--false positives, blind alleys, and

Probably not. 'Robots that can develop humanlike intelligence are far from becoming a reality...[AI] still belongs in the realm of science fiction.'[26]

Ask Noreen Herzfeld. As mentioned above, Herzfeld is both a professor of computer science and a theologian. She provides detail on the question of artificial intelligence in an article elsewhere in this volume. After six to seven decades of attempting to construct a machine with intelligence, she notes, the accomplishment rate is zero. 'We do not yet have intelligent computers. We may never have them.'[27]

Since the term *artificial intelligence* was coined in 1955 by John McCarthy, the concept has been gradually refined. Some distinguish between weak AI and strong AI. Weak AI or narrow AI consists of harnessing the speed of machine computation for a specific or narrow task. Nobody is particularly bothered by the manufacture and distribution of weak AI gadgets.

What about strong AI? The goal of the strong AI movement, in contrast, is to create *artificial general intelligence* (AGI)—that is, a machine capable of performing any task the human brain can perform. Strong AI is classically defined as 'interactive, autonomous, self-learning agency, which enables computational artifacts to perform tasks that otherwise would require human intelligence to be executed successfully'.[28]

The model for strong AI to emulate is human intelligence.[29] Strong AI'ers want to design a robotic competitor, or even superintelligence

---

mistakes...and wasted scientific effort'. Patrick Riley, 'Three pitfalls to avoid in machine learning', in *Nature* 572: 7767 (1 August 2019): 17–19, at 17.

26. Diana Kwon, 'Self-Taught Robots', in *Scientific American* 318:3 (March 2018): 26–31, at 31. With the advent of quantum computers, what can we expect? More speed. Greater capacity. But not intelligence. 'Quantum computers are a not-yet-existent technology in search of problems to solve', Editors, 'Computer games', in *Nature* 564:7736 (20/27 December 2018): 302.
27. Noreen L Herzfeld, *In Our Image: Artificial Intelligence and the Human Spirit* (Minneapolis: Fortress Press, 2002), 94.
28. Mariarosaria Taddeo and Luciano Floridi, 'How AI can be a force for good', in *Science* 361:6404 (24 August 2018): 751–752, at 751.
29. In my own study, I find definitions of 'intelligence' rare. Rather, levels of intelligence seems to be the target of discussion. I launch the thesis that biological life and intelligence belong together. 'Where There's Life There's Intelligence', in *What is Life? On Earth and Beyond*, edited by Andreas Losch (Cambridge UK: Cambridge University Press, 2017): 236–259. See also: Ted Peters, 'Intelligence:

in the form of a machine superior to *Homo sapiens* in calculating capacity, creativity, and awareness. To date, nothing.

Herzfeld notes that this challenge has led many in the field to attempt to construct true AGI by reverse engineering the human brain. Current attempts such as MIT's Mind Machine Project, the US BRAIN Initiative, and the European Union's Human Brain Project are trying to map the connectome of the brain in much the same way the Human Genome Project (1990–2002) successfully mapped human DNA. Even though the Human Genome project was a large and expensive undertaking, reverse engineering the human brain would be even more difficult. It is estimated that the brain contains roughly 80 to 90 billion neurons, each of which can potentially be connected to thousands of other neurons.[30]

This method of reverse engineering what is biological to make an electronic emulation, note, does not begin with a theory of machine intelligence. Rather, what nature through evolution has bequeathed *Homo sapiens* becomes a model to copy. This method begins with a biologically wet brain and then attempts to create a dry electronic copy. With this method, could we reasonably expect the design of a post-human superintelligence? Or, at most, a replication or simulation of what we have inherited from our biological evolution?

Scholastic theologians thought that the creator would necessarily be more complex and more intelligent than what gets created. 'No effect exceeds its cause', said Thomas Aquinas.[31] This implies that God is more complex and more intelligent than us creatures. Might this classic theological principle of causation apply to today's human AI creators? Are we limited to creating robots dumber than we are? If so, does this lessen the Frankenfear?

Can the Dry Machine Brain Mimic the Wet Human Brain?

As of this date, the model of intelligence Strong AI'ers and AGI'ers wish to emulate belongs to the human brain, mind, and self. As the frontier of AI research and development progresses, so also does neu-

Not Artificial, But the Real Thing!', *Theology and Science* 17:1 (February 2019): 1–5; DOI: 10.1080/14746700.2018.1557376.
30. See: Noreen Herzfeld, 'The Enchangment of Artificial Intelligence', elsewhere in this volume.
31. Thomas Aquinas, *Summa Theologica*, II-II, 32, 4, obj 1

roscience and our knowledge of the human brain. Let's pause to parse some of the implications for awareness, consciousness, and selfhood.

We know from experience that our wet brain intelligence is integral to awareness, consciousness, and selfhood. Would this apply to machine intelligence as well?[32] Before pressing further, however, we should distinguish between general awareness and consciousness. Beyond awareness, we who are conscious experience our self as a Self. Might an intelligent robot develop a Self? According to the phenomenology of Eugene d'Aquili and Andrew Newberg, 'Strictly speaking, consciousness involves the generation of a Self as an element in subjective awareness.'[33] If AI is modeled on human intelligence, then we must ask about selfhood.

To date, no computer exhibits selfhood. If you try to relate personally to anything with the label 'Artificial Intelligence', you'll quickly become aware that nobody's home. Even so, we must speculate.

Is a future robot likely to generate first awareness and then a Self? The answer is not yet clear. 'As with the brain, so with artificial intelligence . . . However much we study the complexities of neuro-epistemology, the relationship of consciousness of subjective awareness to the machine, any machine, is a mystery and likely to remain so.'[34] In short, no one at this point can forecast what machine selfhood might look like.[35]

---

32. In *What Computers Still Can't Do: A Critique of Artificial Intelligence* (Cambridge MA: MIT Press, revised edition, 1992), University of California at Berkeley philosopher, Hubert L Dreyphus, denies that a digital computation device could become intelligent in the Strong AI sense. Strong AI could not, in principle, mimic human intelligence. The human intelligence we know is always physically embedded; so intelligence is contextually relevant even while it expands to larger circles of relevance. 'To learn a natural language a computer has to have a body; it must be embodied to be embedded.' *What Computers Still Can't Do*, 181.Dreyfus' prognostication pre-dates the era of computer deep learning. Deep learning machines at this point are unpredictable. What might happen?

33. Eugene G D'Aquili and Andrew B Newberg, 'Consciousness and the Machine', in *Zygon* 31:2 (June 1996): 235–252, at 239.

34. D'Aquili and Newberg, 'Consciousness and the Machine', 251.

35. Could a robot pass the Turing Test and appear to be a self when engaging a human person who is a self? Perhaps. 'Critics of Artificial Intelligence claim that a machine will never have a capacity for self-reflection; in other words, it will always lack a sense of self . . . But . . . it is perfectly viable to elaborate an algorithmic program that allows the machine to report its own internal states. This seems to be a sufficient criterion to affirm that a machine can indeed have

In addition, we need to factor in embodiment and relationality. Human intelligence as we have come to know it is biological and communal. Would this apply to robotic intelligence too? According to the school of *Embodied AI*, 'it is impossible to abstract intelligence from bodily features and bodily conditions'.[36] Impossible?

Theologian Anne Foerst, formerly an AI researcher at MIT working on the Cog project, holds to a relationalist model of the *imago Dei*. The *imago Dei* is not a superior quality we as a species possess such as reason, freedom, moral capacity, love, or virtue. Rather, we humans bear the divine image because God has promised us an everlasting relationship in the Kingdom of God.

This relationalist model implies that we cannot rely on an innate human quality to distinguish us from other living creatures or from artificially constructed creatures. 'The image of God does not distinguish us qualitatively from animals and, for that reason, cannot distinguish us qualitatively from machines.'[37] To say it another way, one could construct a robot with embodied intelligence that is relational and capable of developing a sense of self over time. In the future, we may be invited to dinner by robots in the neighborhood.

Both AI research and neuroscience are consistent with biblical anthropology, according to Ian Barbour.

> Recent work in neuroscience is consistent with the biblical emphasis on embodiment, emotions, and the social self . . . The biblical view does indeed conflict with the determinist and materialist philosophical assumptions of many neuroscientists but not, I suggest, with the data and theories of neuroscience itself.[38]

---

an inner sense of reflection.' Gabriel Andrate, 'Philosophical Difficulties of Mind Uploading as a Medical Technology', in *Philosophy and Medicine* 18:1 (Fall 2018): 14–29, at 17; https://www.academia.edu/37633487/Philosophical_Difficulties_of_Mind_Uploading_as_a_Medical_Technology (accessed 10/23/2018).

36. Anne Foerst, 'Cog, a Humanoid Robot, and the Question of the Image of God', *Zygon* 33:1 (March 1998): 91–112, at 100.
37. Foerst, 'Cog, a Humanoid Robot, and the Question of the Image of God', 108.
38. Ian G. Barbour, 'Neuroscience, Artificial Intelligence, and Human Nature: Theological and Philosophical Reflections', in *Zygon* 34:3 (September 1999): 361–398, at 374.

So far, so good. What remains to be discerned is whether all these traits could in the future apply to a hybrid or even a fully mechanical robot, to artificial intelligence.

More. Might this artificial intelligence become superintelligence? Might the current generation of techie whizzes create a superintelligence which surpasses our biological inheritance? Will our hybrid and mechanical children be smarter than us who gave them existence? If so, will our children revere us as their creators or discard us as outdated?

Regardless of the likelihood that human intelligence will be surpassed by machine superintelligence, theologians and others should feel responsible for speculating about its implications. Trans-humanistså–both religious and anti-religious—are already planning for a future transformation into a world where the post-human dominates.

Bill Joy has issued a warning: 'Our most powerful twenty-first century technologies—robotics, genetic engineering, and nanotech—are threatening to make humans an endangered species.'[39] Anticipation of the extinction of the human species to make way for a new post-human species becomes, for some, an existential threat. It prompts anxiety. To this long range challenge we now turn.

Posthuman Superintelligence?

'High-performance computing is set to soon overtake the human brain', writes Paul Davies.[40] Davies forecasts a future where wet human brains will be replaced by dry computational machines. 'We can now foresee a tipping point when this longstanding relationship between the biological and non-biological realms will become inverted. Instead of life forms such as humans designing and making specialized machines, machines will design and make specialized life forms.'[41] Following the inversion, we *Homo sapiens* will exist only if the machines we create to be our overlords will allow it. More than likely we will go extinct while a species of our disembodied posthuman progeny survive.

---

39. Joy, 'Why the Future Doesn't Need Us'.
40. Paul Davies, *The Eerie Silence: Renewing Our Search for Alien Intelligence* (Boston: Houghton Miflin Harcourt, 2010) 157.
41. Ibid, 160.

In the lexicon of the transhumanists, whole brain emulation will lead to this human, or better, post-human existence, disembodied and living in the computer cloud. "Post-human minds will lead to a different future and we will be better as we merge with our technology," touts Henrique Jorge. 'Humans will be able to upload their entire minds to The Living Cyberspace and BECOME IMMORTAL.'[42]

In the lexicon of Natasha Vita-More, Executive Director of Humanity + Incorporated, *Post-human* refers to 'a person who can co-exist in multiple substrates, such as the physical world as a biological or semi-biological being. The future human . . . will live much longer than [today's] human and most likely travel outside the Earth's orbit.'[43] Does *post-human* describe what will survive after today's *Homo sapiens* have gone extinct?

Anticipation of extinction combined with survival of a species more fit than us in intelligence implies evolution. It implies deep time and a totalistic vision. Today's transhumanists (abbreviated H+) work within the evolutionary paradigm and emphasize that through technology the human race can now both guide and speed up evolution.[44] 'We are about to abandon natural selection, the process that created us, in order to direct our own evolution by volitional selection—the process of redesigning our biology and human nature as we wish them to be.'[45]

The next stage in evolution will be called the 'Singularity', a threshold crossing where superintelligence will replace current intelligence. The first step to get to that threshold is to give birth to a machine more intelligent than us humans. That machine, in turn, will create one still more intelligent. Then the *intelligence ratchet* will take control of procreation and continue the chain of ratcheting up the level of intelligence, crossing the Singularity threshold.

---

42. Henrique Jorge, 'Digital Eternity', *The Transhumanism Handbook*, edited by Newton Lee (Heidelberg: Springer, 2019), 645–650, at 650.
43. Natasha Vita-More, *Transhumanism: What is it?* (published by author, 2018) 31.
44. Nick Bostrom, 'What is Transhumanism?' https://nickbostrom.com/tra/values.html (accessed 10/19/2019). 'Transhumanism is no dogmatic, rigid philosophy with a fixed system of thought or goals defined once and for all. Instead it is a conglomerate of different memes which fit rather well together and support each other without competing too much.' Max More, 'Philosophy', http://www.aleph.se/Trans/Cultural/Philosophy/ (accessed 9/10/2018).
45. Edward O. Wilson, *The Meaning of Human Existence* (London: W.W. Norton, 2014) 14.

With the creation of 'superhuman intelligence . . . the human era will be ended', wrote science fiction writer Vernor Vinge in 1992. This threshold crossing he described as the *Singularity*, when AI becomes awake. The 'Singularity . . . is a point where our old models must be discarded and a new reality rules'.[46]

Computer scientist Ray Kurzweil prophecies that the Singularity will occur as early as 2045.[47] Leading up to the Singularity we will see how the pace of technological change will be so rapid and its impact so deep that human life will be irreversibly transformed.

The nose on this transformation face will be enhanced human intelligence. What follows this nose is the observation that human intelligence will leap from human bodies to machines, making high tech machines more human than we are. This can happen because—allegedly!— intelligence is not dependent upon our biological substrate; rather, as information in patterns, intelligence can be extricated from our bodies. Our intelligence can live on in an enhanced form even when extricated from our bodies and placed in a computer. 'Uploading a human brain means scanning all of its salient details and then reinstantiating those details into a suitably powerful computational substrate. This process would capture a person's entire personality, memory, skills, and history'.[48] Postbiological intelligence will live on in the computer cloud and, as long as no one pulls the plug, it will live

---

46. Verner Vinge, 'What is the Singularity', (1992) https://mindstalk.net/vinge/vinge-sing.html (accessed 9/10/2018).

47. Ray Kurzweil, *The Singularity is Near: When Humans Transcend Biology* (New York: Penguin, 2005), 136. 'The Singularity movement is a kind of secular religion promoting its on apocalyptic and messianic vision of the end times.' William Grassie, "Millennialism at the Singularity: Reflections on the Limits of Ray Kurzweil's Exponential Logic". *H+ Transhumanism and Its Critics,* edited by Gregory R Hansell and William Grassie (Philadelphia: Metanexus, 2011), 249–269, at 264.

48. Kurzweil, *Singularity*, 198–199.

everlastingly.[49] Nothing short of disembodied cybernetic immortality will have been achieved.[50]

Crossing the threshold into the Singularity is nested within a grand evolutionary vision, a vision that makes the technosapiens of our generation godlike.

> Evolution moves toward greater complexity, greater elegance, greater knowledge, greater intelligence, greater beauty, greater creativity, and greater levels of subtle attributes such as love . . . In every monotheistic tradition, God is likewise described as all of these qualities . . . evolution moves inexorably toward this conception of God, although never quite reaching this ideal.[51]

As creators of our own successors, this makes our generation *Homo Deus*. Well, almost.

---

49. What can we expect to happen once our intelligence replete with sense of self is uploaded into the computer cloud? Knowledge would be communal and vast. The history of physical interactions which had converged to establish one's self through time would gradually dissipate. 'My sense of self depends upon memories and continued experiences of those in relation to whom I am defined; deny me access to those memories and those others, and my sense of self would quickly dissolve', John Puddefoot, 'The Last Parochialism? Artificial Life, Intelligence and Mind: Some Theological Issues', in *God, Life, Intelligence and the Universe*, edited by Terence J Kelly, SJ, and Hilary D Regan (Adelaide: Australian Theological Forum, 2002), 111–140, at 133.

50. Is disembodied subjectivity conceivable? Yes, according to biologist and theologian Lucas Mix. 'Rational, subjective, and spiritual life may occur outside of conventional biology. Recent work on artificial intelligence and memes challenges us to think about the meaning of these concepts beyond traditional bounds. Historical reflection on angels, demons, stars, planets, and gods can provide key insights into how we can and should think about 'life' beyond the vegetable context', Lucas John Mix, *Life Concepts from Aristotle to Darwin: On Vegetable Souls* (New York: Macmillan, Palgrave, 2018), 255–256.

51. Kurzweil, *Singularity*, 389. 'Modern transhumanism is a statement of disappointment. Transhumans regard or bodies as sadly inadequate, limited by our physiognomy, which restricts our brain power, our strength and, worst of all, or life span. Transcendence will not be found in the murky afterlife of the usual religions, but in technological and biological improvement', Brian Alexander, *Rapture: How Biotech Became the New Religion* (New York: Basic Books, 2003), 51.

Could Anything Go Wrong?

Transhumanism is 'the most dangerous idea in the world', says social critic Francis Fukuyama.[52] Why? Could something go wrong? Once our transhumanist friends have led us to the top of the Tower of Babel, might we fall off? Are there any risks here?

Like the Sorcerer's Apprentice, might our AI inventions get out of control? The editors of *Nature,* one of the two most important scientific journals in the world today, issue a warning.

> Machines and robots that outperform humans across the board could self-improve beyond our control—and their interests might not align with ours . . . Then there are cybersecurity threats to smart cities, infrastructure and industries that become over dependent on AI—and the all too clear threat that drones and other autonomous offensive weapons systems will allow machines to make lethal decisions alone . . . The spectre of permanent mass unemployment, and increased inequality that hits harder along lines of class, race and gender, is perhaps all too real . . . It is crucial that progress in technology is matched by solid, well-funded research to anticipate the scenarios it could bring about, and to study possible political and economic reforms that will allow those usurped by machinery to contribute to society. If that is a Luddite perspective, then so be it.[53]

According to Stanford computer scientist Stuart Russell, 'the real problem relates to the possibility that AI may become incredibly good at achieving something other than what we really want'.[54] To deal with the problem, Russell recommends that we carefully design the robot; 'the machine's purpose must be to maximize the realization of human values. In particular, the machine has no purpose of its own and no

52. Francis Fukuyama, 'Transhumanism: The World's Most Dangerous Idea', in *Foreign Policy* 144 (2004): 42–43.
53. Editors, 'Anticipating artificial intelligence', in *Nature* 532:7600 (28 April 2016): 413; http://www.nature.com/search?date_range=last_30_days&journal=nature%2Cnews&q=Anticipating%20Artificial%20Intelligence.
54. Stuart Russell, 'Should We Fear Supersmart Robots?', in *Scientific American* 314:6 (June 2016): 58–9 (58); http://www.scientificamerican.com/article/should-we-fear-supersmart-robots/.

innate desire to protect itself'.[55] Somewhat like an ancient emperor trying to prevent a slave rebellion, we *Homo sapiens* can protect our species from a robot revolution only by designing them with a servant mind-set. But, let's pause to ask: would creating robots as our servants really protect us?

Let's pursue this argument another step. Into what servant mind-set would we most likely press our robots? Quite obviously, we will press our AI progeny into the service of our desires. Will that protect us from a robot rebellion? Not likely. Why? Because our artificially intelligent children may simply mirror ourselves, and we rightly fear ourselves.

Brian Patrick Green holds up that mirror.

> Artificial intelligence, like any other technology, will just give us more of what we already want . . . What skeleton of humanity will remain when technology has given us, or perhaps distorted or replaced, all our fleshly desires? What will this skeleton of humanity be made of? Will our technological flesh truly satisfy us, or only leave us in a deeper existential malaise, filled with angst, despair, and dread?[56]

In sum, what we should fear about our AI future is ourselves coming back to us in AI form.

There is one more angle: beyond the Singularity we might become servants to super computers. Our AI progeny might need to keep us around. Why? Because we *Homo sapiens* might be able to offer something super computers cannot do on their own, namely, benefit from diversity of opinion in cultural evolution. Here is the speculation of Neil Levy at Macquarie University in Sydney.

> We owe our intellectual capacities very significantly to our cumulative culture. Culturally embedded cognition allows us to distribute cognition across groups, allowing problems to be broken down into parts, with each solved separately and for our cognitive limitations to be transformed into virtues . . . For this reason, we ought to be wary of thinking that super-

55. Russell, 'Should We Fear Supersmart Robots?', 59.
56. Green, 'Ethical Reflections on Artificial Intelligence', 18.

intelligent machines will have a longer, more extensive, reach
than we do, in virtue of their intelligence.[57]

Superintelligent AIs will need us humans for their own growth intelligence, because the diversity of dynamic human cultures converge
into a single *cultural ratchet*. 'The cultural ratchet may indeed provide
an opportunity for AIs to increase their problem-solving capacities
beyond our current levels, but in so doing it may allow us to increase
our own capacities to the same extent.'[58] In short, we human beings
will end up being of cultural value to our AI overlords.

Anticipating the risk that something could go wrong or that we
might become servants to overlords we create reminds us of the classic myth of Prometheus and his modern heir, Frankenstein. Ian Barbour waves the danger flag. 'The dangers of human *hubris* and misuse
of technological power (evident in myths from Prometheus and the
Tower of Babel to Frankenstein) need exploration.'[59]

Should we Fear Prometheus and Frankenstein?

Might there be a risk here of the Frankenstein scenario?[60] Might the
creation of immortality through technology risk creating a monster?
Might the pursuit of utopia through technology inadvertently lead to
oblivion? Might it be prudent at this point to recall the myth of Prometheus in its modern scientized form of Frankenstein?

Certain scientists prompt whisperings with alarming words such
as *hubris*, or *playing god*, or *Frankenstein*. When you hear these words,
you know that the myth of Prometheus is being retrieved. When 'the
masters of science sought immortality and power', warned Mary
Shelly in 1818, an uncontrollably violent monster was threatening.[61]
Today's Prometheus wears a white lab coat and plans for the future

57. Neil Levy, 'The Earthling's Secret Weapon: Cumulative Culture and the
    Singularity', in *Science, Religion and Culture* 3:1 (2016): 19–30, at 27, Levy's
    italics; file:///C:/Users/Ted/Downloads/1468597863SRC_3_1_19-30%20(3).pdf.
58. Levy, 'The Earthling's Secret Weapon: Cumulative Culture and the Singularity',
59. Barbour, 'Neuroscience, Artificial Intelligence, and Human Nature', 380.
60. See: Ted Peters, 'Playing God with Frankenstein', in *Theology and Science*
    16:2 (2018): 145–150; DOI: 10.1080/14746700.2018.1455264; https://www.
    tandfonline.com/doi/full/10.1080/14746700.2018.1455264.
61. Mary Shelly, *Frankenstein: The Modern Prometheus* (New York: Pocket Books,
    1818, 2004), 43.

(*pro-mathein* means to think ahead). Today's threatening monsters come in the form of environmental degradation, climate change, engineering tomatoes with fish genes, genetically engineering the highly lethal H5N1 influenza, cloning Dolly the Sheep, transplanting pig organs into humans, and global nuclear war. These worries are affectionately known as *Frankenfears.*

It was Prometheus who is responsible for today's Frankenfears. Returning briefly to ancient Greek writers such as Hesiod and Aeschylus, the Titan Prometheus did two things worth recalling. First, Prometheus created the human race, forming our ancestors out of clay. Second, he stole fire from the sun and gave fire to us creatures living on an otherwise dark and damp Earth. Prometheus' gift of fire led to human advance in writing, mathematics, agriculture, medicine, and science. But, this theft violated the sanctity of the heavens overseen by the Olympian god, Zeus. In anger, Zeus retaliated by chaining Prometheus to a rock. The imprisoned Prometheus helplessly endured the indignity and pain of having an eagle, the symbol of Zeus, daily eat his liver. For trespassing against the sanctity of the divine realm, Prometheus was punished by the gods.

This myth cannot be consigned to the dead past. It lives today. Prometheus winds his way through the centuries of historical transmission (*Wirkungsgeschichte, Überlieferungsgeschichte*). We today still associate Prometheus with *hubris,* pride, overstepping our limits, crossing into forbidden territory, and violating the sacred. The antidote to Promethean recklessness is humility, caution, and sound judgment. Sometimes when we fear Promethean overreach, we put up an ethical stop sign that reads, 'Thou shalt not play god'.

Mary Shelly intended for us to see Prometheus again in Frankenstein. Victor Frankenstein's sin was to play god, to attempt to create life out of non-life. 'Life and death appeared to me ideal bounds, which I should first break through, and pour a torrent of light into our dark world. A new species would bless me as its creator and source; many happy and excellent natures would owe their being to me.'[62] The scientist in this story tried to apotheosize himself by creating, like Prometheus did, his own living creature who would laud him as divine. But, says author Shelly, this action violated what was

---

62. Shelly, *Frankenstein: The Modern Prometheus*, 51.

sacred and the sacred, like Zeus, retaliated by letting loose a monster on the world.

Recall how the monster and Victor Frankenstein argued over the *imago Dei*, the image of God twice removed. The lonely creature confronted his maker. 'Cursed creator! Why did you form a monster so hideous that even you turned from me in disgust? God in pity made man beautiful and alluring, after his own image; but my form is a filthy type of yours, more horrid from its very resemblance. Satan had his companions, fellow-devils to admire and encourage him; but I am solitary and detested.' [63] The creature would not have suffered loneliness nor the neighbors suffered havoc had Victor Frankenstein not played god.

Today, when we accuse our scientists of 'playing god', we accuse them of violating the sacred. But, what is sacred? No modern person believes in Zeus any more. So, Mount Olympus cannot establish the sacred. What about the biblical God? The Promethean myth is not biblical. Nothing in the Bible forbids scientific advance into the sacred. So, what counts as the violated sacred? Here is the answer: nature. In the modern world nature has replaced Zeus as the sacred. To violate nature is to risk nature's retaliation, to risk letting a monster loose on the world.[64]

With all the warnings we've inherited from the Tower of Babel, Prometheus, and Frankenstein, we would expect that today's religious sensibilities would prompt us to wince and flinch at transhumanism. Certainly no religious person could place a stamp of approval on this bald attempt to storm heaven on a technological ladder. Right? Wrong. Religious transhumanists are sprouting up like dandelions after a spring rain.

AI and Religion! Really?

An AI Church? That's what Anthony Levandowski, former executive at Google and Uber, is planning. He plans to name the church *The Way of the Future;*, and his holy scripture will take the form of *The Manuel*. When the superintelligent robots we humans create become

---

63. Shelly, *Frankenstein: The Modern Prometheus*, 154.
64. See: Ted Peters, *Playing God? Genetic Determinism and Human Freedom* (London: Routledge, 2nd ed., 2003).

smarter than we are, then we'll need to treat them as gods. So, we may as well get into the habit of appeasing our new gods now.[65]

> Levandowski believes that humans dominate the world because we evolved to be more intelligent than other animals; in the same way, AI will eventually supersede the power of its creators. It will be so much more intelligent than us that it will, effectively, become a god. With the Internet as its nervous system, the world's connected cellphones and sensors as its sense organs, and data centers as its brain, this new deity will be as omniscient and omnipotent as any previous vision of God. In the face of such power, Levandowski believes, humans will merely submit and pray to be spared.[66]

Elsewhere we're watching the rise of new syncretisms between otherwise atheistic transhumanism and religious visionaries.[67] As of this writing we can list Buddhist transhumanism,[68] Unitarian Universalist transhumanism,[69] Mormon transhumanism, and even versions of

65. Kif Leswing, 'Ex-Google executive Anthony Levandowski is founding a church where people worship an artificial intelligence god', in *Business Insider* (November 16, 2018) https://www.businessinsider.com.au/anthony-levandowski-way-of-the-future-church-where-people-worship-ai-god-2017-11.

66. Galen Beebe and Zachery Davis, 'When Silicon Valley Gets Religion--and Vice Versa', in *Boston Globe* (November 7, 2018) https://www.bostonglobe.com/ideas/2018/11/07/when-silicon-valley-gets-religion-and-vice-versa/L5xOYtgwd4VImwcj52YxtK/story.html.

67. See: Ted Peters, 'Boarding the Transhumanist Train: How Far Should the Christian Ride?', in *Transhumanism Handbook,* 795-804. DOI 978-3-030-16920-6_62.

68. Michael LaTorra, "What is Buddhist Transhumanism?" *Theology and Science* 13:2 (2015) 219-229. A syncretism of H+ with Islam is unlikely. 'While the modern movement towards transhumanism aims to improve sensory perception by way of scientific intervention, Islamic transhumanism calls on believers to improve and purify their perceptions by way of God-consciousness, brought about increasing in remembrance of God. It might be argued that a Muslim's transhumanist goals are directly tied to their devotion to God, rather than mastery of secular science. This difference embodies the fundamental difference between an Islamic transhumanism and secular transhumanism.' Tamim Mobayed, 'Immortality on Earth? Transhumanism Through Islamic Lenses', in *Yaqeen* (December 11, 2017); https://yaqeeninstitute.org/en/tamim-mobayed/immortality-on-earth-transhumanism-through-islamic-lenses/.

69. James Hughes, 'Transhumanism and Unitarian Universalism: Beginning the Dialogue', (2005), http://changesurfer.com/Bud/UUTrans.html.

Christian transhumanism.[70] Lincoln Cannon, erudite spokesperson for Mormon transhumanism, lifts up an inspiring vision.

> As transhumanists, we have discarded the old assumption that human nature is or ever was static—not only because science has demonstrated biological evolution, but especially because history itself is cultural and technological evolution . . . humanity will continue to evolve. Our common ambition is to inject ourselves into the evolutionary process, changing our bodies and minds, our relationships, and even our world for the better--perhaps to learn, love, and create together indefinitely . . . Mormon transhumanism stands for the idea that humanity should learn how to be God; and not just any kind of god, not a god that would raise itself in hubris above others, but rather the God that would raise each other together as compassionate creators. Humanity should learn how to be Christ."[71]

The evolution of superintelligence converges, for such religious visionaries, with divinely promised transformation. Science and technology become the means for sanctification if not deification and more. There seems to be no essentialist Ludditism or Frankenfear at work in Lincoln Cannon.

However, an Eastern Orthodox theologian, Ian Curran, waves the flag of Frankenfear caution. First, deification does not mean each human being becomes a god; rather, it means flowing fully into the life of the one and only God. Second, deification could not be the product of human technological progress.

> While the Christian tradition does share with techno-humanism a vision of deification as integral to the human story, its understanding of the source, means, and ultimate end of this radical transformation of human beings is

---

70. Christian Transhumanist Association, http://changesurfer.com/Bud/UUTrans.html (accessed 10/20/2018). Sympathetic Christian critics are also at work. Ronald Cole-Turner, 'Going Beyond the Human: Christians and Other Transhumanists', in *Theology and Science* 13:2 (2015): 150–161; Brian Patrick Green, 'Transhumanism and Roman Catholicism: Imagined and Real Tensions', in *Theology and Science* 13:2 (2015): 187–201.
71. Lincoln Cannon, 'What is Mormon Transhumanism?', in *Theology and Science* 13:2 (May 2015): 202–218 (202–203).

> substantially different. For Christians, deification is the work
> of the Christian deity . . . Deification is only possible because
> Christ deifies human nature in the incarnation and the Spirit
> sanctifies human persons in the common life of the church
> and in our engagements with the wider world.[72]

Ultimate deification requires divine grace. Technological advance belongs strictly in the penultimate domain. H+ contributes nothing to sanctification or deification.

Could we split the middle between Lincoln Cannon's extravagant hybridization of secular H+ with Mormon H+, on the one end of the spectrum, and Ian Curran's complete rejection of H+ on the other? Might there be a moderate theological position based upon a moderate variant of transhumanism? Here is what a moderate H+ looks like, according to a Roman Catholic theologian at Ruhr-Universität Bochum, Germany, Benedikt Paul Göcke.

> According to the moderate transhumanist agenda, it is
> morally valuable to enhance the human nature of individual
> subjects, externally and internally, and where it is possible
> permanently, through the use of applied science, in order to
> increase their range of human physical and mental capacities
> with respect to an objective scale of measurement of physical
> and mental abilities that are judged to be good for human
> subjects to have.[73]

With this in mind, Göcke argues that Christians can in principle fully endorse the transhumanist agenda because there is nothing in Christian faith that is in contradiction to it. In fact, given certain plausible moral assumptions, Christians should endorse a moderate enhancement of human nature."[74]

If H+ were a seducer and religion the damsel, the Mormon would accept a marriage proposal; the Orthodox would refuse all romantic dinner invitations; and the Roman Catholic would enjoy the flirting.

---

72. Ian Curran, 'Becoming godlike? The Incarnation and the Challenge of Transhumanism', in *Christian Century* 134:24 (November 22, 2017): 22–25, at 25.
73. Benedikt Paul Göcke, 'Christian Cyborgs: A Plea for a Moderate Transhumanism', in *Faith and Philosophy* 34:3 (2017): 347–364, at 352.
74. 'Christian Cyborgs: A Plea for a Moderate Transhumanism', 347.

Conclusion

It should be tacitly clear that the transhumanist movement represents the prow of the modern Western ship as it sails toward the colonization of the mind just as in previous centuries it colonized human bodies. If H+ dreams come true, a new elite will emerge in cities the world over, an elite made up of those with access to superintelligence. H+ is not an egalitarian ideology, by any means. Nor is there a likelihood that H+ will invite previously marginalized peoples into its techtopia.

In addition to the justice question, theologians will ask about anxiety. Weak AI elicits no anxiety when intelligence is confined to mentally challenged robots busy vacuuming the living room rug. Nor are artists upset when computers paint portraits. Even factory workers, tempted to worry at the prospect of losing their jobs to robots, expectantly search for more high-tech employment.

When it comes to Strong AI or AGI, however, anxiety begins to rise. Strong AI compels us to ask existential questions such as: what does it mean to be human? Will our human species go extinct so that a more fit post-human species can survive? So, what is our intelligence anyway?

History teaches us that the future will not be neat, clean, orderly. It will be disruptive. Things can and will go wrong.[75] Will the Sorcerer's Apprentice go wild? Will our superintelligent children treat outdated *Homo sapiens* dismissively or even cruelly? Is there good reason for Frankenfear?

Despite transhumanist claims of a utopian transformation wrought by scientific and technological progress, a healthy Frankenfear or at least a caution is warranted. We know from the truths about

---

75. Christians should keep the doctrine of sin handy when trying to accomodate Transhumanism. 'The Christian cosmology of the redemptive Gospel cannot be reconciled with a metaphysical and philosophical system reliant upon endless evolutionary complexification. The Christian must ask (and be prepared to explain) what it means to the transhumanist to be human and we must also be prepared to expose the sin-side of their plans. For while there may be much good in longer life, sin remains and sin is prone to ruin good things and the good life so many pursue. We have to face the fact that people—even highly evolved people—have done, are doing and will continue to do horrible things.' Carmen Fowler LaBerge, 'Christian? Transhumanist? A Christian Primer for Engaging Transhumanism', in *Transhumanism Handbook*, 771–776, at 775.

human nature revealed to us in the stories of the Tower of Babel (Gen 11:1–9), Prometheus, and Frankenstein that utopian aspirations risk creating monsters that get out of control. In the case of transhumanism, that monster could lead to oblivion for the human species. Even without an uncontrollable monster, human oblivion is part of the H+ plan.

I forecast that byproducts of neuroscientific research and attempts to build ever smarter computers will benefit the human race. These sciences and resulting technologies will likely improve medical care and may even increase human longevity. Nevertheless, a healthy caution if not full Frankenfear of utopian promises is warranted by the doctrine of sin reinforced by historical knowledge about how the human race behaves. A sinful humanity is incapable of creating a sinless superintelligence. Utopia is not possible by human effort alone.

The ultimate transformation Christians look forward to is eschatological. It will be a gift of divine grace. John Polkinghorne reminds us of this. 'An ultimate hope will have to rest in an ultimate reality, that is to say, in the eternal God himself, and not in his creation.'[76] It would behoove the present generation to view AI advance as penultimate, not ultimate. A healthy dose of Frankencaution is warranted.

---

76. John Polkinghorne, *The Faith of a Physicist* (Princeton NJ: Princeton University Press, 1994), 163.

Somnambulating Towards AI Dystopia?
The Future of Rights and Freedoms

Neville Rochow

"The real problem relates to the possibility that AI may become incredibly good at achieving something other than what we really want."
– Stuart Russell[1]

Abstract. Dystopia is familiar to us. It is close to our daily lived experience with technology and Amazon, Apple, Facebook, and Google (the Four). The Four and AI pose an existential risk. History teaches that supranational corporations cannot be trusted with unchecked power or to respect human rights. With the combination of AI and the Four, our situation is akin to Rawls' 'original position' behind a 'veil of ignorance'. None can predict the effect AI will have on human rights. We should take our rights seriously before the bio-technological lottery begins. Prompt international action is required to regulate AI developers and corporations.

Key Words. Artificial Intelligence, corporations, human rights,

Bio. Neville Rochow SC, LLB (Hons), LLM, (Adelaide), LLM (Deakin) is a senior barrister who holds an adjunct associate professorship at Adelaide Law School. He has practised in areas of commercial, corporate, and constitutional law. Currently, he is writing a PhD thesis that explores the constitutional limits of freedoms of conscience and religion.

In Yevgeny Zamyatin's 1924 novel *We,*[2] OneState controls the planet. Happiness is guaranteed to all Numbers, the inhabitants of this future

---

1. Stuart Russell, 'Should We Fear Supersmart Robots?', in *Scientific American,* 314/6 (June 2016): 58–59 (58); http://www.scientificamerican.com/article/should-we-fear-supersmart-robots/.
2. Written in Russian and published in various languages beginning with English in 1924.

world, by OneSate's scientific method, the Table of Hours. The Table is drawn by Zamyatin from the efficiency theories of Frederick Taylor[3] and the Soviet management practices of Nadezhda Krupskaya.[4] It prescribes every Number's activity at every moment of each day. The success of OneState project is underwritten by the Benefactor, who is supported in surveillance and enforcement performed by the Bureau of Guardians. OneSate's control is absolute.

The story begins with a *State Gazette* writing project. Entries are to be sent to uncharted planets. Numbers are to 'place the beneficial yoke of reason round the necks of unknown beings who inhabit other planets—still living, in the primitive state known as freedom'.[5] Our narrator, D-503, a rocket scientist, contributes his entry in the form of a series of 'records'. In one 'record', D-503 muses on this quaint twentieth century notion, 'freedom':

> I've read and heard a lot of unbelievable stuff about those times when people lived in freedom—that is, in disorganised wildness. But of all things the every hardest for me to believe was how the governmental power of that time, even if it was still embryonic, could have permitted people to live without even a semblance of our Table . . . It's so funny, so improbable, that now I've written it I am afraid that you, my unknown readers, will think I'm making wicked jokes . . . [but] OneState Science cannot make a mistake. [If freedom were to manifest itself] . . . These are fortunately no more than little chance details; it's easy to repair them without bringing to a halt the great eternal progress of the whole Machine.[6]

The distant future world of *We* seems all too familiar. Part of that familiarity derives from the popular trope in film and literary fiction of a post-apocalyptic dystopian future[7]. Two striking commonalities

---

3. Clarence Brown, 'Introduction: *Zamyatin and the Persian Rooster*', in *We*, Yevgeny Zamyatin, translated by Clarence Brown (Penguin Group, 1992), xviii.
4. Brown, 'Introduction: *Zamyatin and the Persian Rooster*', 1.
5. Brown, 'Introduction: *Zamyatin and the Persian Rooster*', 1, 3.
6. Brown, 'Introduction: *Zamyatin and the Persian Rooster*', 3, 13–15.
7. Examples from film include *Metropolis* (Fritz Lang, 1927), *Blade Runner* (Ridley Scott, 1982), *Blade Runner 2049*, (Denis Villeneuve, 2017), *AI* (Steven Spielberg, 2001) and *Minority Report* (Steven Spielberg, 2002). Examples of dystopian literature (much of which has been turned into film) include *The Time Machine* (1895) by HG Wells, *Lord of the World* (1908) by Robert Hugh Benson, *RUR:*

recur in the trope: a presence and an absence. Commonly *present* in the trope is the pervasiveness of technology, regulating every activity, often exploited for totalitarian purposes by a mysterious government or megacorporation.[8] Noticeably *absent* are basic human rights and freedoms, including conscience, religion, belief, association, and expression.

Life Imitates Art

Life imitates art. *We* is also familiar in our domestic and working lives. Today, technology rules us. Daily, we imbibe a mix of artificial intelligence[9] (AI), intelligence amplification[10] (IA), robotics[11], and corporate power.[12] Four supranational corporations, with unri-

---

Rossum's Universal Robots (1921) by Karel Čapek, *We* (1921, Russian, 1924, English) by Yevgeny Zamyatin, *Brave New World* (1932) by Aldous Huxley, *It Can't Happen Here* (1935) by Sinclair Lewis, *Animal Farm* (1945) by George Orwell, *Nineteen Eighty-Four* (1949) by George Orwell, *Utopia 14* (1952) by Kurt Vonnegut, *Fahrenheit 451* (1953) by Ray Bradbury, *Minority Report* (1956) by Philip K Dick, and *The Man in the High Castle* by Philip K Dick (1962).

8. As in *I, Robot* (Alex Proyas, 2004). See also Elizabeth Anderson, *Private Government – How Employers Rule Our Lives (and Why We Don't Talk about It)* (Princeton University Press, 2017).

9. Machine intelligence, or intelligence demonstrated by machines, in contrast to the natural intelligence displayed by humans. For discussions of its manifestation, see: Scott Galloway, *The Four – The Hidden DNA of Amazon, Apple, Google and Facebook*, (2017, Transworld Publishers), chapter 1 and 196–200; Richard Susskind and Daniel Susskind, *The Future of the Professions – How Technology Will Transform the Work of Human Experts* (2015, 2017, Oxford University Press), chapters 1 and 2.

10. Yuval Noah Harari, *Homo Deus – A Brief History of Tomorrow* (2014, Harvill Secker), 353–359 (described as 'techno-humanism'; Galloway, *The Four – The Hidden DNA of Amazon, Apple,* note 9, above. See also Francis Fukuyama, *Our Posthuman Future – Consequences of the Biotechnology Revolution* (2002, Picador).

11. 'Robotics' as used here includes design, construction, operation, and any use of robots; and computer systems used for their control; and information processing. Regarding Amazon's use to replace human work see Galloway, *The Four – The Hidden DNA of Amazon, Apple,* note 9, above, at 52–54.

12. Galloway, *The Four – The Hidden DNA of Amazon, Apple,* note 9, above, at 54–57; Robert Verbruggen, 'Google, Facebook, Amazon: Our Digital Overlords', 12 December 2017, *Nation Review* at https://www.nationalreview.com/2017/12/google-facebook-amazon-big-tech-becoming-problem; James Heskett, 'Is It

valled international market power, control most of our technology: Amazon; Apple; Facebook; and Google, ('the Four').[13] Each possesses the strategic economic power of a nation-state.[14] They decide if, how, and where they are to be regulated;[15] what market practices they will employ; if when, where, and how much tax they pay; what, if any, ethical standards they will implement. Imposition of fines is merely an operational cost.[16] Most importantly, into the future, they will effectively decide what, if any, human rights they will respect and the extent to which it suits their overriding profit motive.

Technology insinuates itself into our every activity. We gormlessly accept the toxic elixir of corporate power and technological addiction without question as to the harm that may be done. Scarcely a thought is given to the motives and methods of the formless behemoths that provide it. In short, we take our chances. Instead of questioning, with unstinting trust, we confide our personal and financial details so that we can continue to receive good and services from the Four. If we considered the security breaches of which they are guilty, the unemployment they cause, and the control they seek over us for profit, we would regard them as vice. They should be viewed, as Alexander Pope described, monsters of 'frightful mien'.[17]

Time To Break Up Amazon, Apple, Facebook, or Google?' 6 December 2017, *Working Knowledge Business Research for Business Leaders*, Harvard Business School, at https://hbswk.hbs.edu/item/is-it-time-to-break-up-amazon-apple-facebook-or-google?cid=wk-rss.

13. James Heskett, 'Is It Time to Break Up Amazon, Apple, Facebook, or Google?'. 'Supranational' is used here to describe corporations, like the Four, who have substantial economic and technological power sufficient to transcend states and their control and to submit, effectively, when convenient. 'Transnational' describes and corporation or business that trades across national borders.

14. Anderson, *Private Government – How Employers Rule Our Lives*, note 7 above; Galloway, *The Four – The Hidden DNA of Amazon, Apple*, note 9, above.

15. Verbruggen, Google, Facebook, Amazon: Our Digital Overlords', note 11 above.

16. Luigi Zingales, 'How E.U.'s Google Fine Explains High Cellphone Costs in the U.S.', 24 July 2018, *The New York Times*, at https://www.nytimes.com/2018/07/24/opinion/european-union-google-fine-monopoly.html

17. *Essay on Man*, Epistle II:
    Vice is a monster of so frightful mien,
    As, to be hated, needs but to be seen;
    Yet seen too oft, familiar with her face,
    We first endure, then pity, then embrace.

Rather than hating[18] as Pope advised[19], we have become *familiar*[20] with the Four in our homes and offices; we *endure*[21] their affinity algorithms[22] and eavesdropping devices[23]; we *pity* Zuckerberg when he is publicly humiliated over Facebook's misuse of personal information[24]; we just *embrace* new gadgets and services that we do not need; and we continue to accept the convenience of Amazon's supply chain. It does not seem to trouble us that Amazon replaces 76,000 employees annually with robots.[25] Apple is venerated when it defies a Federal Court order to assist in a mass murder investigation.[26] Facebook's misuse of data for profit[27] and photographs for facial recognition[28] changes none of our social media habits permanently. Despite Google being fined a record 4.34 billion Euros for anti-competitive conduct in the EU;[29] we continue to trust its answers to all our questions.

---

18. *Essay on Man.*
19. *Essay on Man.*
20. *Essay on Man.*
21. *Essay on Man.*
22. Galloway, *The Four – The Hidden DNA of Amazon, Apple*, note 9, above, at 105 – 114.
23. Eric Limer, 'Hundreds of Apps Can Eavesdrop Through Phone Microphones to Target Ads', 3 January 2018, *Popular Mechanics*, at https://www.popularmechanics.com/technology/security/a14533262/alphonso-audio-ad-targeting/
24. Galloway, *The Four – The Hidden DNA of Amazon, Apple*, note 9, above, at 107, regarding the Cambridge Analytica scandal.
25. Galloway, *The Four – The Hidden DNA of Amazon, Apple*, note 9, above, at 29–30, 52–54.
26. Galloway, *The Four – The Hidden DNA of Amazon, Apple*, note 9, above, at 63–66.
27. See note 23 above and Jessica Guynn, 'Facebook wants to save your face. Should you say yes to facial recognition?' 19 April, 2018 *USA TODAY*, at https://www.usatoday.com/story/tech/news/2018/04/19/facebook-growing-use-facial-recognition-raises-privacy-concerns/526937002/
28. Zingales, 'How E.U.'s Google Fine Explains High Cellphone Costs in the U.S.', note 16, above.
29. Zingales, 'How E.U.'s Google Fine Explains High Cellphone Costs in the U.S.'; Adam Satariano and Jack Nicas, July 18, 2018, 'E.U. Fines Google $5.1 Billion in Android Antitrust Case', *The New York Times* at https://www.nytimes.com/2018/07/18/technology/google-eu-android-fine.html

Questions Without Answers

Why do we take such chances? Because we consider the promises to be greater than the risks. The 'fourth industrial revolution'[30], promise a cornucopia of low-cost, high quality goods and services supplied in miraculously short time by unseen algorithms and robotic minions. These technological servants meet consumers' every want and need, at their beck and call. Information will be available in unimaginable volumes and at mind-blistering rates. We will think faster with artificial enhancements and increase our physical capabilities with robotic exoskeletons and extensions. Efficiencies will optimise with inventions yet to be imagined. Gadgets we once considered unthinkable outside of science fiction are now with us: the 'internet of things';[31] nanotechnological manufacture;[32] driverless cars;[33] and intelligent commercial and domestic accommodation.[34] Agriculture is becoming less susceptible to climate changes through the development of new plant and animal breeds.[35] With medical advances, genetic attributes of offspring will be made to order;[36] ailments will be detected

---

30. Generally used to describe the fourth major industrial period since the Industrial Revolution of the eighteenth century, involving electronic, digital, and robotic technologies and frequently merging the physical, digital, and biological capacities. See: Klaus Schwab, *The Fourth Industrial Revolution* (2017, New York: Crown Publishing Group); Callum Chace, *The Economic Singularity: Artificial Intelligence and the Death of Capitalism* (2016, The Three Cs).

31. See Schwab, *The Fourth Industrial Revolution,* note 30, above; Steve Ranger, 'What is the IoT? Everything you need to know about the Internet of Things right now Updated: The Internet of Things explained. What the IoT is, and where it's going next.' 21August, 2018, ZDNET, at https://www.zdnet.com/article/what-is-the-internet-of-things-everything-you-need-to-know-about-the-iot-right-now/

32. Nanoscience and nanotechnology are the study and application of extremely small things and can be used across all the other science fields, such as chemistry, biology, physics, materials science, and engineering: https://www.nano.gov/nanotech-101/what/definition

33. See Google's website for its driverless car project, Waymo: https://waymo.com/

34. See Intelligent Buildings at https://www.intelligentbuildings.com/#scroll-get-started

35. See the CSIRO project for marker assisted breeding to isolate desirable genotypes in specific environmental and climatic conditions: https://www.csiro.au/en/Research/Farming-food/Innovation-and-technology-for-the-future/Gene-technology/Marker-breeding

36. Harari, *Homo Deus – A Brief History of Tomorrow,* note 10, above, at 52–54.

early,[37] monitored remotely,[38] and treated prophylactically;[39] longevity will be at the individual's discretion.[40] The environment could well benefit from technologies that will minimise our carbon footprint[41] and possibly even reverse some destructive effects from the first three industrial revolutions.[42]

The Fourth Industrial Revolution

This fourth industrial revolution also promises to usher in unprecedented social change.[43] As with any revolution, the scale and nature of change remains all but impossible to predict[44]. Cherished hopes for this imminent utopia are closely bound to our deepest fears.[45] The combination of AI, IA, and robotics conjures a new force that is at once a genie-like slave for those whose lives are enriched and a sinister usurper for those whose employment will be rendered redundant. Will the professions survive the new outpouring upon the general population of what was once arcane knowledge reserved

37. Amy Jeter Hansen, 'Artificial intelligence in medicine — predicting patient outcomes and beyond' 8 May 2018, Scope, Stanford Medicine, at https://scopeblog.stanford.edu/2018/05/08/artificial-intelligence-in-medicine-predicting-patient-outcomes-and-beyond/; Alvin Rajkomar et al 'Scalable and accurate deep learning with electronic health records', *npj Digital Medicine* volume 1, Article number: 18 (2018), at https://www.nature.com/articles/s41746-018-0029-1; See also Fukuyama, *Our Posthuman Future*, note 10, above at 70–71.
38. See note 37, above.
39. See note 37, above. See also Harari, *Homo Deus – A Brief History of Tomorrow*, note 10, above, at 5, 25–27, 32–34, 50.
40. Harari, *Homo Deus – A Brief History of Tomorrow*, note 10, above, at 5, 25–27, 32–34, 50; See also Fukuyama, *Our Posthuman Future*, note 10, above at 70–71.
41. Jane Burston, 'Four technological innovations that can help reduce urban carbon emissions' 6 June 2016.
Horizons Smart Cities, at https://www.citymetric.com/horizons/four-technological-innovations-can-help-reduce-urban-carbon-emissions-2103
42. Jahda Swanborough, 'The previous industrial revolutions broke the environment. Can the current one fix it?', 20 April 2017, *World Economic Forum*, at https://www.weforum.org/agenda/2017/04/fix-the-environment-there-s-an-app-for-that/
43. See note 30, above. See also James Barrat, *Our Final Invention: Artificial Intelligence and the End of the Human Era*,
44. See Fukuyama, *Our Posthuman Future*, note 10, above.
45. Fukuyama, *Our Posthuman Future*, note 10, above. See also Barrat, *Our Final Invention*, note 44, above, chapters 3, 10, and 14.

for specialists?[46] How will those with manual skills be re-deployed?[47] What new economic and political balances will need to be struck? What will be the effect on real estate when business and governmental space is no longer required? How will demographics shift if only some sectors of the population have the privilege of aging healthily and gracefully? How will humans, transhumans, and androids inter-relate? In whose image will the new emergent society be re-shaped? Could the promised utopia be the dystopia of science fiction?

To see the apocalyptic potential that threatens, we need not trace back two hundred years to *Frankenstein,*[48] or through twentieth century works of Zamyatin, George Orwell, Aldous Huxley, and Philip K Dick,[49] and the whole genre of unwitting creators and faceless organisations unleashing technology-gone-horribly-wrong. Writers and filmmakers of this century[50] continue warn regarding our political, economic, and ethical destiny in a world in which science and corporations rule supreme. But that body of artistic works is now joined by a rich expert literature posing precisely the same questions;[51] ethical and moral questions posed but that remain unanswered.[52] At heart,

---

46. See Susskind, *The Future of the Professions*, note 9, above. See also Richard Susskind, *Tomorrow's Lawyers – An Introduction to Your Future* (2017, Oxford University Press, 2nd ed.)
47. Susskind, *The Future of the.*
48. *Frankenstein, or the Modern Prometheus* by Mary Shelley (1818).
49. See note 7, above.
50. See notes 7 and 8, above.
51. Apart from works previously cited, see: Nick Bostrom, *Superintelligence - Paths Dangers, Strategies* (2014, Oxford University Press); Siva Vaidhyanathan, *The Googlization of Everything* (2012, University of California Press); Siva Vaidhyanathan, *anti-social media – How Facebook Disconnects Us and Undermines Democracy* (2018, Oxford University Press); Kevin Kelly, *The Inevitable: Understanding 12 Technological Forces That Will Shape Our Future* (2016, Penguin Books); Kevin D Ashley, *Artificial Intelligence and Legal Analytics – New Tools for Law Practice in the Digital Age* (2017, Cambridge University Press); Max Tegmark, *Life 3.0 – Being Human in the Age of Artificial Intelligence* (2017, Penguin Books); Franklin Foer, *World Without Mind – The Existential Threat of Big Tech* (2017, Penguin Press); Lasse Rouhiainen, *Artificial Intelligence – 101 Things You Must Know Today About Our Future* (2018, Lasse Rouhiainen).
52. David J Gunkel, *The Machine Question – Critical Perspectives on AI, Robots, and Ethics* (2017, MIT Press); Jesse Russell and Ronald Cohn, *Ethics of Artificial Intelligence* (2012, Lennex Corp). See also Ana Beduschi, 'Technology dominates our lives – that's why we should teach human rights law to software engineers', 26 September 2018, The Conversation, at https://theconversation.com/technology-

one dilemma is just how are we to offset our insatiable desire for progress against the preservation of rights and freedoms that define our humanity? How do we avoid the potential dystopian hell?

So, which is it going to be—utopia or dystopia? Rarely do the purveyors of the dystopian trope explain either the attainment of technological supremacy or the loss of basic rights. As in a dream gone awry, along with the fictional protagonists, we are dropped in the middle of the unfolding nightmare with no explanation as to just how all of this came about. In one rhapsodic variation on the nightmare,[53] the plot devolves from utopian technology behaving as the humans' compliant servant, to that disastrously unanticipated moment of machine self-will that translates into chaos. The computer or robot usurps control from hapless humans to become the malevolent master. The pivot in the plot is driven by a belated insight: some self-absorbing malware had somehow stealthily crept into the programming. That insight comes all too late for the subjugated humans. They become victims of, literally, inhuman treatment. Until control is regained by the scripted remnant, the technology displays ruthless disregard for its erstwhile masters.

Many questions remain unanswered. Many more are yet to be asked.

The Pollyanna and Cassandra Syndromes

We have had more than our share of wrong predictions. Failing to sign Elvis Presley, the Beatles, or JK Rowling, forecasting the First World War to last only a few months, the predicted collapse of modern technology on 1 January 2000 with the Y2K bug, and Francis Fukuyama's vaunting of capitalism as the End of History,[54] have, each in their way, fuelled a cynicism for human predictive powers. Our cynicism couples with our inability to discern correct predictions when they are

---

dominates-our-lives-thats-why-we-should-teach-human-rights-law-to-software-engineers-102530?utm

53. For example, in film, *2001 – A Space Odyssey*, (Stanley Kubrick, 1968) and *Saturn 3* (Stanley Donen, 1980). In literature, *Frankenstein* remains possibly one of the best examples.

54. Francis Fukuyama, *The End of History and the Last Man* (1992, Free Press)

made: the bombing of Pearl Harbor;[55] global terrorism;[56] that Bernie Madoff's Ponzi scheme would collapse.[57] Our innate tendency is towards believing those with optimistic messages and the least effort, the Pollyannas. We hope that doomsayers, the Cassandras, who may be right, will prove to be wrong and that the efforts they advocate will be unnecessary.[58] So, we ignore the (potential) Cassandras and follow the Pollyannas.

Be careful of the companies we keep

We tend to overlook inherent flaws in corporations and AI. We attribute to them human qualities but exclude flaws and imperfection. These attributions are merely simulacra. Even the legal personality of a corporation is a legal fiction and limited in purpose. Both the corporation and AI are human creations that inherit human failings in their design, production, and operation. Human bias is present in input and output.

The 'failings' factor should influence us to have more respect for those Cassandras who may just be likely right on AI and corporations. We should take the chance that they are right rather than they are wrong. Predictions range through the paradisaical,[59] the benign,[60] to the cataclysmically disastrous.[61] But looking to the origins, there is cause for healthy disrespect. Both the corporation, especially supranational corporations, and AI have terrible pedigrees.

On the unknowable potential of corporations, in his insightful work, *The Corporation – The Pathological of Pursuit of Profit and Power*, Joel Bakan observes:

---

55. Barbara Tuchman, *The Zimmerman Telegram* (2014, Random House).
56. Brynjar Lia, *Globalisation and the Future of Terrorism, Patterns and Prediction* (2005, Routledge).
57. Peter Sander, *Madoff – Corruption, Deceit, and the Making of the World's Most Notorious Ponzi Scheme* (2009, The Lyons Press), 96–105.
58. Cassandra, blessed with the gift of accurate prophecy, was cursed that her prophecies would not be believed. See Homer's *Iliad*, Book XXIV, lines 820–830.
59. See discussion of Google's Ray Kurtzweil in Barrat, *op. cit.*, at note 43, 28–31.
60. Susskind, Susskind, *Tomorrow's Lawyers*, at note 10.
61. See Bostrom, Foer, Vaidhyanathan, and Tegmark, cited at note 51, above.

When in 1933, Supreme Court Justice Louis Brandeis likened corporations to 'Frankenstein's monster',[62] there was more to his observation than rhetorical flair. Governments create corporations, much like Dr Frankenstein created his monster, yet, once they exist, corporations threaten to overpower their creators.[63]

The pedigree of the supranational corporation traces back to 1543 and the creation of a proto-corporation, the Church of England. It was used as the vehicle for Henry VIII's reverse takeover of the Catholic Church in the English Reformation.[64] State-power was invested in the new Church. Henry, as its head, through the new Church, cut all ties to the Vatican, dried up its income streams by abolishing indulgences, appropriated income and assets of the monasteries, and thus substantially increased the wealth of the English Crown. In the enterprise, Henry was ruthless in his pursuit of an ultimately futile ambition—gaining a male heir. He regarded life, conscience, and property rights as irrelevant in that pursuit. He executed anyone that stood in his way.

The Honourable East India Company (HEIC or East India Company), the first supranational trading corporation, received its Royal Charter in 1600 from Henry's heir, Elizabeth I. HEIC eclipsed Henry in rapacity and disregard for property. In pursuit of markets, capital, and profit, it showed no respect for borders, sovereignty, or the rights of nations or individuals. HEIC colonised India, and, using private armies, took control of all trade and commerce, and installed British government in place of indigenous fiefdoms. To secure monopoly

62. *Louis K Liggett Co v Lee*, 288 U.S. 517, 564–67 (1933) (Brandeis, J, dissenting in part). Justice Brandeis borrowed the phrase from Maurice Wormser, *Frankenstein, Incorporated* (1931). Discussed in Robert N Strassfeldt, 'Introduction: Corporations and Their Communities', *Case Western Reserve Law Review* Vol. 58:4 1017 (2008) at 1019.
63. Joel Bakan, *The Corporation – The Pathological of Pursuit of Profit and Power* (2005, Constable), 149.
64. Christopher Hill, 'Social and Economic Consequences of the Henrician Reformation', in *Puritanism & Revolution -Studies in Interpretation of the English Revolution* (1958, 2001, Pimlico), 30–45.

trade in China's tea, it did not scruple at gunboats and addiction to opium.[65]

Corporations, to varying extents, have since emulated the East India Company's actions to secure markets, monopolise, and profit by whatever means at their disposal.[66] Examples include: the *Banque Générale* and the Company of the West, both of which, under the direction of John Law, contributed as causes of the French Revolution;[67] the Dutch East India Company, which enabled Holland's conquest of the Dutch East Indies and monopolisation of the spice trade;[68] the Hudson's Bay Company, which monopolised trade in Canadian resources;[69] the Rothschild firm[70], which speculated in national and international wars for profit;[71] Rockefeller's Standard Oil, which, with other trust corporations, throttled the economy of mid-nineteenth century United States;[72] Microsoft Corporation, which stymied national and international software markets through

---

65. Philip J Stern, *The Company-State: Corporate Sovereignty & the Early Modern Foundations of the British Empire in India* (Oxford University Press, 2011); John Keay, *The Honourable Company: A History of the English East India Company* (Harper Collins Publishers, 1991); John Keay, *India, A History: From the Earliest Civilsations to the Boom of the Twenty-First Century* (Harper Press, 2010);

66. *Company* (Harper Collins Publishers, 1991); John Keay, *India, A History: From the Earliest Civilsations to the Boom of the Twenty-First Century,* above n 62, 28–60 and 111 *et seq*. See also: Yuval Noah Harari, *Sapiens – A Brief History or Humankind,* Penguin (Random House UK, 2011), 31–36; Niall Ferguson, *Empire: How Britain Made the Modern World* (Penguin Group, 2003); John Micklethwait and Adrian Woolridge, *The Company: A Short History of a Revolutionary Idea* (Phoenix, 2003); and Nick Robins, *The Corporation That Changed the World: How the East India Company Shaped the Modern Multinational* (Pluto Press, 2nd ed, 2012). See also note 65, above.

67. Niall Ferguson, *The Ascent of Money: A Financial History of the World* (Penguin Group, 2008), 139–158.

68. Ferguson, *The Ascent of Money: A Financial History of the World*, 129-138.

69. HBC Heritage, 'Our History: Overview' (October 2015) <http://www.hbcheritage.ca/history>.

70. While not necessarily corporations, the operation of the firm was 'supranational' and 'corporate' in every other sense.

71. Ferguson, *The Ascent of Money: A Financial History of the World* above n 66, 79–87, 90–92, 97-98 and 114–115.

72. Ron Chernow, *Titan – The Life of John D. Rockefeller,* Sr, Random House, Inc. 1998, chapter 7; Ida M. Tarbell, *The History of the Standard Oil Company,* (1904 McClure, Phillips and Co.)

anti-competitive practices;[73] the dishonest culture of the four major Australian banks;[74] and, of course, the conduct of the Four.

Superintelligence

On the unknowable potential of technology, in his magisterial work *Superintelligence - Paths Dangers, Strategies*, Nick Bostrom commences with a salutary, but, so far, unfinished parable:

> A group of sparrows are building their nests. 'We are all so small and weak,' tweets one, feebly. "Imagine how easy life would be if we had an owl who could help us build our nests!' There is general twittering agreement among sparrows everywhere; an owl could defend the sparrows! It could look after their old and their young! It could allow them to live a life of leisure and prosperity! With these fantasies in mind, the sparrows can hardly contain their excitement and fly off in search of the swivel-headed saviour who will transform their existence . . .

There is only one voice of dissent:

> Scronkfinkle, a one-eyed sparrow with a fretful temperament, was unconvinced of the wisdom of the endeavour. Quoth he: 'This will surely be our undoing. Should we not give some thought to the art of owl-domestication and owl-taming first, before we bring such a creature into our midst?' His warnings, inevitably, fall on deaf sparrow ears. Owl-taming would be complicated; why not get the owl first and work out the fine details later? . . .'[75]

---

73. *United States v Microsoft Corporation* 253 F.3d 34 (2001).
74. *Interim Report of Royal Commission into Misconduct in the Banking, Superannuation and Financial Services Industry*, 28 September, 2018, at https://financialservices.royalcommission.gov.au/Documents/interim-report/interim-report-volume-1.pdf
75. 'The Unfinished Fable of the Sparrows', (truncated version from Tim Adams, 'Artificial intelligence: 'We're like children playing with a bomb', 12 June 2018, *The Guardian*, at https://www.theguardian.com/technology/2016/jun/12/nick-bostrom-artificial-intelligence-machine The full version is in Bostrom, *Superintelligence - Paths Dangers, Strategies,* note 51, iii–iv.

The ancestry of AI is no less noble than that of the supranational corporation. Machine intelligence traces its origins to one or more of three sources: war; fast food; or pornography.[76] If and when machines reach human intelligence for all purposes,[77] predicted social and economic upheaval include scenarios of realigned stratifications where those can afford to adopt technology as a part of their own biological and cognitive make-up will succeed,[78] while those who cannot will be downtrodden and subjugated. In short, some will be bio-technologically deified[79] while others are dehumanised.[80]

Unregulated corporations with AI, IA, and AGI at their disposal is just not a smart option for humans. Without international norms to guide commercial and military applications of AI, it would seem humanity takes part in a waiting game to see whether the Pollyannas were right.

A New Rawlsian Veil of Ignorance?

We are all now in a situation akin to Rawls' 'original position'[81] behind an actual 'veil of ignorance'.[82] None of us knows what will happen to our rights and freedoms in the short-term with supranationals in control of AI.[83] Neither can we predict what will happen with human rights when AGI occurs or if the event horizon of superintelligence is reached.[84] It is not even possible to predict the sequence in which AGI and superintelligence may arrive.[85] The potential scenarios call

---

76. Peter Nowak, *Sex, Bombs and Burgers – How War, Pornography, and Fast Food Have Shaped Modern Technology* (Viking Canada 2010).
77. Bostrom, *Superintelligence - Paths Dangers, Strategies*, note 51, chapters 3 and 4.
78. Tegmark, *Life 3.0 – Being Human in the Age of Artificial Intelligence*, note 51, 118–133.
79. Harari, *Homo Deus – A Brief History of Tomorrow*, note 10.
80. Harari, *Homo Deus – A Brief History of Tomorrow*, note 10.
81. John Rawls, *A Theory of Justice* (Harvard University Press, revised ed, 1999) chapter 3.
82. Ibid, 118-123.
83. Nick Bostrom, *Superintelligence: Paths Dangers, Strategies* (Oxford University Press, 2014), 4, 22–25, 77, 107, 303--05 and 364.
84. Bostrom, *Superintelligence: Paths Dangers, Strategies*, 130–131, 188 and 378.
85. Bostrom, *Superintelligence: Paths Dangers, Strategies*.

for us to take human rights and freedoms seriously[86] now before the bio-technological lottery begins.

If the predictions ended there, Michael Sandel, in commenting on Rawls,[87] could, of course, be right: some behind this veil of ignorance might still opt to take their chances and continue to ignore human rights. But on the superintelligence scenario, because of the unpredictable nature of the implications for us, the planet, and, indeed, the universe, constraint upon developers and users must enter the equation.[88]

Superintelligence is reached when artificially intelligent machines themselves would write the code and control the production of other artificially intelligent machines.[89] They would be able to network, pool their intelligence, and press into service robotic extensions to manufacture hardware and means of production.[90] This intelligence explosion is one in which humans will necessarily be inferior in intelligence and capability to those possessed by machines. They will be at the mercy of the machines much like inferior species have been at ours throughout human history. There is nothing to constrain this new type of being to behave either beneficently or even benignly disposed towards humans. It could regard with pity and affection, like kindly god, or view us as a source of carbon, minerals, or energy.[91]

If there is to be any chance of avoiding the worst of the predicted scenarios, then the machines that are being designed now must be biased in our favour. Though not a guarantee, not attempting it is a risk that is not worth taking.

---

86. Ronald Dworkin, *Taking Rights Seriously* (Duckworth 1996), 90-94 and 188-192. See also chapters 6 and 7 *passim*.
87. Michael J Sandel, *Justice: What's the Right Thing to do?* (Penguin Group, 2009) chapter 6. Particularly 157–166.
88. Sandel, *Justice: What's the Right Thing to do?*, above n 82, 5, 25, 67, 124–126, 140–154, 220–221, 282–287, 295–302, 315–316, 357 and 378.
89. Sandel, *Justice: What's the Right Thing to do?*, 26, 63–64 and 71.
90. Sandel, *Justice: What's the Right Thing to do?*, 26, 63–64 and 71..
91. Sandel, *Justice: What's the Right Thing to do?*, chapters 7, 8 and 9 *passim* and 364 at note 10.

Bias: The Real Ghost in the Machine

Computer output has effect upon the humans who consume it. If we needed to be reminded of this truism, Selena Scolla, one of Facebook's censors, is suing her employer for the post-traumatic stress disorder caused by content she had to vet in the course of her employment.[92] What is sometimes overlooked is the effect that humans and their biases have in the generation of AI and the use of its output. Bias is, generally, negatively perceived. We want our judges and decision-makers to be fair, impartial, and definitely unbiased. But in machines, it is a different matter.

Alan Turing, arguably, invented not only the computer but also the dilemma of bias. During his pioneering AI work to break the Enigma encryption machine codes, the question was who would receive the data he and the Hut 8 team generated and how and when would it be used?[93] This was a moral and practical dilemma.[94] Unless used with strategic restraint, the Allies' hand would be tipped, and the Germans would know they had broken the code. Too restrained a use would result in avoidable military and civilian casualties. While data input was dictated by the intercepted coded messages, use of output had to be a matter of human judgment and discretion. Human judgment necessarily brings with it bias, even bias of which the assessor is not conscious.

As AI steadily increases its insinuation into more of our daily lives, the question of invisible bias will become increasingly important.[95] For example, the effects of bias upon AI medical triage and dispensation are obvious enough. Apparently binary choices of whether

---

92. Elizabeth Dwoskin, 'Facebook content moderator says she got PTSD while reviewing images' 25 September 2018, *The Sydney Morning Herald*, at https://www.smh.com.au/business/workplace/facebook-content-moderator-says-she-got-ptsd-while-reviewing-images-20180925-p505sg.html
93. See Andrew Hodges, *Alan Turing: The Enigma* (2012, Vintage), chapter 4, 'The Relay Race', *passim* and at 252–255, 275–280, and 301.
94. This was, of course, not a new dilemma in war and espionage. Its novelty was in the machine-generation and the human judgment on use of the output.
95. Pedro Domingos, *The Master Algorithm* (Penguin Random House UK, 2015) 78-79 and chapters 7 and 9. See also Max H Bazerman and Ann E Tenbrunsel, *Blind Spots: Why We Fail to Do What's Right and What to Do about It* (Princeton University Press 2011), 20–21, 81–82, 115–116 and 137; Ajay Agrawal et al, *Prediction Machines: The Simple Economics of Artificial Intelligence* (Harvard Business Review Press, 2018), 34–35, 55–58, 195–198 and 204–205.

to administer treatment or not and whether to prescribe a particular drug may have unseen drivers that tilt the decision-making. Are the choices driven by impartial medical assessments in the best interests of the patient or by undeclared economic imperatives?

The implications of bias to health care are vital. They have great importance in the area of human rights. Largely, human rights actors have been distracted by nice questions of equality and liberty. These questions are insignificant in comparison with the near and present threat that AI poses. Take but one example: the right to freedom of thought, conscience, religion or belief in ICCPR[96] Article 18.[97] What happens when an algorithm decides whether or not to administer a blood transfusion without consideration of the patient's religious beliefs? If no connected algorithm asks a question whether the patient is a faithful Jehovah's Witness, the machine will decide the

---

96. *International Covenant on Civil and Political Rights* (New York, 16 December 1966), Entry into force generally (except Article 41): 23 March 1976, Entry into force for Australia (except Article 41): 13 November 1980, Article 41 came into force generally on 28 March 1979, and for Australia on 28 January 1993

97. Article 18 of the ICCPR provides:
   (1) Everyone shall have the right to freedom of thought, conscience and religion. This right shall include freedom to have or to adopt a religion or belief of his choice, and freedom, either individually or in community with others and in public or private, to manifest his religion or belief in worship, observance, practice and teaching.
   (2) No one shall be subject to coercion which would impair his freedom to have or to adopt a religion or belief of his choice.
   (3) Freedom to manifest one's religion or beliefs may be subject only to such limitations as are prescribed by law and are necessary to protect public safety, order, health or morals or the fundamental rights and freedoms of others.
   (4) The States Parties to the present Covenant undertake to have respect for the liberty of parents and, when applicable, legal guardians to ensure the religious and moral education of their children in conformity with their own convictions.
   Compare Article 9 of the European Covenant on Human Rights:
   (1) Everyone has the right to freedom of thought, conscience and religion; this right includes freedom to change his religion or belief and freedom, either alone or in community with others and in public or private, to manifest his religion or belief, in worship, teaching practice and observance.
   (2) Freedom to manifest one's religion or beliefs shall be subject only to such limitations as are prescribed by law and are necessary in a democratic society in the interests of public safety, for the protection of public order, health or morals, or for the protection of the rights and freedoms of others.

question without reference to religious faith. What if the machine is programmed to have a bias in favour of termination of pregnancies if the patient has measles? If the programmer has not taken any account of Catholic belief on abortion, a termination may result without reference to the patient's beliefs. What if the patient is of a certain age, frailty of health or socio-economic status? If particular social biases in favour of euthanasia have been installed into the machine, then strongly held religious or ethical positions on the part of the patient or their family may be disregarded and the patient euthanised contrary to beliefs and wishes.

Time is running out on these issues. The source codes and algorithms for these decisions to be made are being written now and being sold by transnational corporations to consumers of AI in in numerous jurisdictions. Chances are that any programmer is unlikely to be familiar with First Amendment jurisprudence, the terms of Article 18, or human rights norms, let alone have read the moral and political philosophies of Aristotle, Hobbes, Locke, Bentham, Mills, Kant, Rawls, Dworkin, or Sandel. Their default positions in writing the source code, interpreting output, or making judgments based upon output will be more likely determined first, by the relevant law, then, secondly, by corporate policy, and, if there remain gaps, according to their own biases.

Australia: Far Too Little and Much Too Late

Just how ill-prepared the world is for the fourth industrial revolution and its human rights implications is illustrated by two contrasting jurisdictions: Australia (the least prepared) and the European Union (EU) (the most advanced jurisdiction in AI policy). Australia is the only advanced economy in the Western world not to have a national bill or charter of rights.[98] There remains a debate as to whether there should be a bill of rights at all.[99]

---

98. For the position on the State of Victoria and the Australian Capital Territory, see Alistair Pound and Kylie Evans, *An Annotated Guide to the Victorian Charter of Human Rights and Responsibilities* (Thomson Lawbook Co, 2008); and Carolyn Evans and Simon Evans, *Australian Bills of Rights* (LexisNexis Butterworths, 2008).

99. See Neville Rochow, *Paying for Human Rights Before the Bill Comes: Towards a More Comprehensive Domestic Implementation of International Human Rights*

Australia is currently inquiring into various economic and social issues.[100] In those inquiries that touch upon either AI or human rights, there appears no rush to either report on findings or implement recommendations. The ACCC inquiry, for example, into digital platforms is not due to deliver its final report until June 2019.[101] This current inquiry seems to be a response to the ACCC's unsuccessful 2013 legal action against Google,[102] takes no account of Moore's Law:[103]

Norms in Australia, University of Adelaide Law School. (2009), available at http://ssrn.com/abstract=1356382; Paul Babie and Neville Rochow (eds) *Freedom of Religion Under Bills of Rights* (2012, University of Adelaide Press), available at https://www.adelaide.edu.au/press/titles/freedom-religion/; Julian Leeser and Ryan Haddrick (eds), *Don't leave us with the Bill: the case against an Australian Bill of Rights* (2006, Menzies Research Centre).

100. Recent and current Royal Commissions include:
   - Royal Commission into Institutional Responses to Child Sexual Abuse (2013–2017)
   - Royal Commission into Misconduct in the Banking, Superannuation and Financial Services Industry (2017–present)
   - Royal Commission into aged care quality and safety (2018-Present)
   Other recent and current inquiries include:
   - Department of Prime Minster and Cabinet Religious Freedom Review (the Ruddock Inquiry) https://www.pmc.gov.au/domestic-policy/religious-freedom-review
   - Australian Competition and Consumer Commission (ACCC) Digital platforms inquiry https://www.accc.gov.au/focus-areas/inquiries/digital-platforms-inquiry
   - Australian Human Rights Commission (AHRC) Human Rights and Technology inquiry.humanrights.gov.au/our-work/rights-and-freedoms/projects/human-rights-and-technology https://www.humanrights.gov.au/our-work/rights-and-freedoms/projects/human-rights-and-technology

101. Timeline: Terms of reference: 4 December 2017; Issues paper: 26 February 2018; Submissions: 3 May 2018; Forums: 15 August 2018. The preliminary report is to be submitted to the Treasurer by 3 December 2018, with a final report due by 3 June 2019: https://www.accc.gov.au/focus-areas/inquiries/digital-platforms-inquiry

102. *Google Inc v Australian Competition and Consumer Commission* [2013] HCA 1; (2013) 249 CLR 435. http://eresources.hcourt.gov.au/showCase/2013/HCA/1 See discussion in Amanda Scardamaglia and Angela Daly 'What consumers need from the ACCC inquiry into Google and Facebook', *The Conversation*, at https://theconversation.com/what-consumers-need-from-the-accc-inquiry-into-google-and-facebook-88560

103. Simply put, overall processing power for computers will double every two years. This formulation is now dated. It also takes no account of progression from binary processing to quantum molecular processing. See discussions at http://

by the time the inquiry is completed, it will almost certainly be historical in relation to the operations of the IT corporations and how AI affects consumers.

To take another example, the Ruddock inquiry, which examined the need for legislation to protect freedom of religion in Australia, reported on 18 May 2018. At the time of writing, the federal government is yet to make that report public.[104] It is still unknown whether inquiry has recommended legislative protection for freedom of religion.[105]

Recall that Australia has no national bill of rights.[106] Despite that lack, the AHRC, a body with oversight over the limited Australian human rights regime, held a 'Human Rights and Technology' conference on 24 July 2018 to launch an issues paper to discuss the following:

- The right to equality and non-discrimination;
- Freedom of expression;
- Right to benefit from scientific progress;
- Freedom from violence;
- Accessibility for people with disability;
- Right to privacy;
- Right to education;
- Access to information and safety for children; and
- Right to a fair trial and procedural fairness[107]

---

www.mooreslaw.org/ and https://www.research.ibm.com/ibm-q/learn/what-is-quantum-computing/

104. Katharine Murphy, 'Kerryn Phelps urges PM to release Ruddock religious freedom review before byelection', 26 September 2018, *The Guardian*, at https://www.theguardian.com/australia-news/2018/sep/26/kerryn-phelps-urges-pm-to-release-ruddock-religious-freedom-review-before-byelection?CMP=share_btn_link

105. https://www.pmc.gov.au/news-centre/domestic-policy/statement-panel

106. Instead, it has a patchwork of state laws and the following pieces of federal legislation:
    - *Australian Human Rights Commission Act 1986*
    - *Age Discrimination Act 2004*
    - *Disability Discrimination Act 1992*
    - *Racial Discrimination Act 1975*
    - *Sex Discrimination Act 1984*

107. https://tech.humanrights.gov.au/conference

One notices immediately that freedom of religion or belief is not included among the discussion topics. This is possibly because there is no current federal legislation protecting freedom of religion.[108]Another obvious omission is how the Four and other IT corporations that utilise AI could be required to respect human rights in Australia. Speakers did include Microsoft's Steve Crown[109] and Google's John Lucchi.[110] Both were reassuring regarding their respective corporation's human rights credentials and intentions. To paraphrase Mandy Rice-Davies,[111] they would say that, wouldn't they?

Another item that might have been discussed was the potential use of blockchain technology[112] to guarantee that all AI, IA, AGI, and (it would be hoped) Superintelligence has been encoded, designed, and engineered with human rights protections.[113] A globally distributed human rights ledger of rights as a pre-requisite to the use of every peer-to-peer network would be a basic start to the protection of human rights into the fourth industrial revolution.

But, it would seem, Australia struggles to get to the first stage in protecting human rights. When it does, it may well be a case of far too little and much too late.

---

108. There is a very limited protection in the federal Constitution at s. 116. See discussions in: Luke Beck, *Religious Freedom and the Australian Constitution: Origins and Future*, (2018, Routledge) chapters 6 - 12; Paul Babie, Joshua Neoh, James Krumery-Quinn, Chong Tsang, *Religion and Law in Australia* (2015, Wolters Kluwer), Part I, chapter 1, and Part II, chapter 2.

109. Vice President and Deputy General Counsel, Human Rights, Microsoft Corporation.

110. Head of Content and AI, Public Policy and Government Relations, Google Asia Pacific.

111. Geoffrey Robertson, 'Mandy Rice-Davies: fabled player in a very British scandal', 19 December 2014, *the Guardian* at https://www.theguardian.com/politics/2014/dec/19/mandy-rice-davies-fabled-player-british-scandal-profumo

112. Derek Parker, 'How governments are using blockchain technology', 22 August 2018, *INTHEBLACK*, at https://www.intheblack.com/articles/2018/08/22/how-governments-using-blockchain-technology

113. As was discussed at the Artificial Intelligence in Legal Practice Summit 2018 hosted by the College of Law on 31 August 2018: https://www.cli.collaw.com/events-and-workshops/2018/02/01/artificial-intelligence-in-legal-practice-summit-2018

EU and 'Hate Speech' Regulation – A Leap of Faith?

The EU is the most advanced jurisdiction in AI policy, ethics, law, and practice,[114]with a dedicated parliamentary platform[115] and a specialised section of the European Commission working towards a Digital Single Market.[116] The Commission has developed legal and ethical frameworks to ensure that the EU is ahead of technological developments and encouraging uptake by the public and private sectors and that all members states are prepared for the socio-economic changes brought about by AI.[117]

On 10 April 2018, 25 European countries, including member states of the EU, signed a multi-lateral Declaration of cooperation on AI. On the declaration, Andrus Ansip, Vice-President for the Digital Single Market, and Mariya Gabriel, Commissioner for Digital Economy and Society, showed that the Europeans have recognised what most other national governments have failed to see:

> In Europe, any successful strategy dealing with AI needs to be cross-border. A large number of Member States agreed to work together on the opportunities and challenges brought by AI. That is excellent news. Cooperation will focus on reinforcing European AI research centres, creating synergies in R&D&I funding schemes across Europe, and exchanging views on the impact of AI on society and the economy. Member States will engage in a continuous dialogue with the Commission, which will act as a facilitator.[118]

The EU has developed a policy on the prevention of online 'hate speech'. In May 2016, Facebook, Twitter, YouTube and Microsoft committed to combatting the spread of such content in Europe through a 'Code of Conduct', implementation of which was to be overseen in a

---

114. Compare the United Nations' *Future of Life Institute*: https://futureoflife.org/ai-policy-united-nations/?cn-reloaded=1
115. The *European AI Alliance*: https://ec.europa.eu/digital-single-market/en/european-ai-alliance
116. https://ec.europa.eu/digital-single-market/
117. https://ec.europa.eu/digital-single-market/en/artificial-intelligence
118. https://ec.europa.eu/digital-single-market/en/news/eu-member-states-sign-cooperate-artificial-intelligence

series of monitoring rounds.[119] The third monitoring round was held on 19 January 2018.[120] Since May 2016, Google had announced it was joining the Code of Conduct, and Facebook confirmed that Instagram would also. One of the challenges found to remain at the third evaluation round was a lack of systematic feedback to users. The third evaluation also found that IT companies removed on average 70% of illegal hate speech notified to them.

At the third evaluation, Věra Jourová, EU Commissioner for Justice, Consumers and Gender Equality, observed on the purposes of the Code of Conduct:

> The Internet must be a safe place, free from illegal hate speech, free from xenophobic and racist content. The Code of Conduct is now proving to be a valuable tool to tackle illegal content quickly and efficiently. This shows that where there is a strong collaboration between technology companies, civil society and policy makers we can get results, and at the same time, preserve freedom of speech. I expect IT companies to show similar determination when working on other important issues, such as the fight with terrorism, or unfavourable terms and conditions for their users.

Despite claims of success for the Code, fundamental questions remain regarding the entire scheme. First, it is not clear what definition of 'hate speech' the IT companies would use in their vetting of alleged breaches. Article 20 (2) of the ICCPR provides that, 'Any advocacy of national, racial or religious hatred that constitutes incitement to discrimination, hostility or violence shall be prohibited by law'. Apart from this, there has been no universally accepted definition of 'hate speech'. The term is not precisely defined by any EU document and the definition in law is also vague.[121]

---

119. https://www.wsj.com/articles/eu-cheers-tech-giants-commitment-to-tackling-online-hate-speech-1496315958
120. http://europa.eu/rapid/press-release_IP-18-261_en.htm
121. Rex Ahdar and Ian Leigh, Religious Freedom in the Liberal State (2013, Oxford University Press, 2nd ed), 448–451; Rona McRea, *Religion and the Public Order* (2010, Oxford University Press), 71–72, 103–140: Paul Coleman, *Censored: How European 'Hate Speech' Laws are Threatening Freedom of Speech* (2016, Kairos Publications, 2nd Ed), chapters 3 and 7; Mike Hume, *Trigger Warning – Is the Fear of Being Offensive Killing Free Speech?* (2015, Williams Collins).

Second are questions of liability:

- who among employees of the corporations make the decisions for users of their services; with what authority? and
- what, if any liability arises and against whom for wrongful removals?

The Code is silent on safeguards and guarantees of the rights of those who wrongfully silenced. There are no appeal processes or avenues for redress.[122]

The third question is why the implementation and enforcement the Code, public cyber-policing roles, have been delegated to supranational corporations. While the answer may lie in pragmatism, when a conflict of interest arises between their own profit motive and the private interests of a user, whose interests ought they to prefer? And how is any conflict of interest dealt with on a day-by-day, case-by-case basis? We can assume of the IT corporations one thing: they would not have entered an agreement to sponsor the Code unless they considered that, in the long run, their interests would be best served by doing so.

So, who watches the watchman? The EU would say that the Commission, NGOs and civil society. But only time will confirm whether that is enough. Thus, the Code, though venerable for its intent, seems to have several risks attached to it, not the least of which, is entrusting so much of the welfare of EU citizens to supranational corporations.

Conclusions

With the exception of games, as humans, we tend not to take chances. Games have an element of chance attached to them. It is the combination of chance, obedience to rules, and demonstration of skill that makes games entertaining. Chance is also an element of our ordinary everyday choices. But the degree of chance tolerable in games is not tolerable in life. Rules are stricter and there are consequences for breach. Skill is often rewarded by increased market demand, but without any guarantee. We tend to be risk-averse in the real world;

---

122. Adina Portaru, 'Freedom of Expression Online: The Code of Conduct on Countering Illegal "Hate Speech" Online', *Revista Romana de Drept European* n. 4/2017, Wolters Kluwer Romania.

our tendency is to minimise risk by taking control of those matters that can be brought within our power. In real life, we tend to seek certainty by having rules enforced and seeking evidence of that those who supply have the skill to deliver.

Yet we still fail to see the threat that the unprecedented power of AI in the hands of supranational corporations poses. Confronted with existential threats from what has been regarded as the virtual world of AI, a world born in science fiction and computer games, we are having a hard time taking those threats seriously. We are taking chances, trusting in skill without evidence, and failing to develop and apply rules. Despite the oncoming threats to our humanity, we still fail to take human rights seriously.

An obvious solution is international application of human rights norms to the writing, design, and engineering of all AI, IA, AGI, and, hopefully, Superintelligence. With blockchain technology, all other advances could come with guarantees of conformity of human rights protections. But the pathway to that solution is thwarted by national silos of domestic law and failures to understand the enormity of the potential outcome. In the meantime, AI and supranational corporations continue unregulated.

Shortly put, if the international community seeks to exploit AI, leaving development to markets and human rights to chance, we face an existential risk. As to the timing and extent of that risk, no-one can predict other than to say that the worst-case scenario is devastation. If the international community cannot agree on how to limit the power of corporations to control AI, the risks are the same. Without immediate international agreement on these issues, the possible Cassandras are warning us of potential catastrophe. In the meantime, that we are somnambulating towards an AI dystopia.

Artificial Intelligence and Intelligence Amplification: Salvation, Extinction, Faulty Assumptions, and Original Sin

Alan Weissenbacher

'Man is insecure and involved in natural contingency; he seeks to overcome his insecurity in a will-to-power which over reaches the limits of human creatureliness.'
– Reinhold Niebuhr[1]

Abstract. In the literature on artificial intelligence one finds predictions that robots will drive the majority of humanity into unemployment or extinction, on the one hand. One the other are predictions that in the techno-future, super-intelligent machines (or humans) will solve all moral and natural evils, leaving humanity free to pursue creative interests while robots provide for all material needs. These predictions, however, contain several faulty assumptions. First, the definition of intelligence is vague and confused, resulting in inappropriate comparisons of human and machine intelligences. Second, there is an implicit assumption that more intelligence equates to greater morality. Related to this is the idea that greater intelligence will bring with it the will to solve society's problems, which is by no means the case. Addressing these assumptions reveals that instead of salvation or extinction (utopia or oblivion), these technological advances represent a new set of benefits as well as challenges to overcome, particularly the tendency of human technical creations to reflect the sins of their creators even under the best of intentions.

Key Words. Artificial Intelligence (AI), Intelligence Amplification (IA), Original Sin, Assumptions, Ethics

Bio. Alan Weissenbacher is book review editor for *Theology and Science*. He served many years as a counselor to homeless addicts, removing them from the urban setting and empowering them to run a farm while receiving coun-

---

1. Reinhold Niebuhr, *The Nature and Destiny of Man*, Gifford Lectures, 2 Volumes (New York, Scribners, 1941), 1:178.

seling, spiritual care, and job training. His work with these clients inspires his research into neuroscience and spiritual formation, exploring ways to improve religious care and addiction recovery through understanding how the brain works.

It is easy to find gloomy predictions that in the near future robots will drive the majority of humanity into unemployment, or worse, result in its extinction. This extinction is possible through an inadvertent mistake such as telling an artificial intelligence (AI) to make paperclips but failing to specify an endpoint so that the whole earth is buried in paperclips, through a deliberate act, such as AI deciding to enslave or rid the world of inferior humans, or as a side-effect such as an AI launching a nuclear strike on a rival AI. At the same time, one finds utopian visions of what an AI driven future can be, despite whatever growing pains society experiences in the meantime.

AI advocates and transhumanists advance the idea that humanity is soon approaching the moment where it makes a machine smarter than itself. This moment is termed 'The Singularity'. Once we cross the Singularity threshold, transhumanists predict we will begin a rapid chain reaction where this machine or program begins to create other, newer versions of itself, each one improving on the last, resulting in machines of vastly superior intelligence.[2] Robots and AI will then perform all tasks efficiently without the need for human labor so that goods will be free and readily available to all. Humans, no longer forced to work, will be able to enjoy lives of leisure devoted to creative pursuits. These super intelligent AIs, or perhaps intellectually enhanced humans, will save the environment, cure disease, and resolve societal ills, assuming that the lack of solutions to these problems to date is purely a result of ignorance. But even if there are other reasons, these are solvable as well since it is expected that a super intelligence will also fix the problems of greed, hate, and other problematic human characteristics. People can then turn running the world over to a benevolent 'AI God' free from human evil. Utopia will have arrived, thanks to AI.

2.   Eliezer Yudkowski, AI researcher, points out the existence of several schools of thought on the singularity, differing on the time frame for advancement and how predictable an AI future will be. Eliezer Yudkowski, 'Three Major Singularity Schools', Machine Intelligence Research Institute, accessed 9/14/2018. www.intelligence.org/2007/09/30/three-major-singularity-schools/.

It is apparent where such predictions come from, as programmers and researchers continually develop skilled AIs that produce impressive results. Computers have bested human opponents in chess, poker, GO, and the TV game show Jeopardy.[3] Self-driving cars have managed to navigate across the United States, and Google gave a media demonstration in May, 2018 of Duplex, an AI assistant that can mimic human voice and speech patterns, including cadence and mannerisms. The demonstration showed that Duplex was able to fool receptionists at a hair salon and restaurant into thinking that they were speaking with a real human. (This also raises the specter of realistic but faked audio and video of world leaders).

This demonstration technically passed the Turing Test, traditionally the gold standard for determining human-like intelligence in a computer. If someone cannot distinguish a machine from a human in conversation, then this computer is to be seen as intelligent. Duplex did just that. While reporting seemed impressed with Duplex as a technical achievement, no one suggested that Duplex actually represented what passing the Turing test should indicate—human-like intelligence. Everyone understood that this was mimicry based on processing the data from thousands of conversations, but it does perhaps suggest the need to reevaluate the Turing test.

It is true that AI will bring societal disruption in the near term, particularly in the area of employment, as many jobs can be automated without strong AI, a machine or program that exhibits intelligence equal or surpassing the human. Weak AI, machine intelligence focused on a narrow task, will suffice. The effects of this near-term disruption cannot be underestimated. Many seem to think that it is only low-skill jobs at risk for automation and that those effected can be retrained into more creative professions.[4] First, skill retraining is problematic, as it is not yet evident what new sills would be 'automation resistant', not to mention that it is expensive to retrain persons later in their working lives. And second, AI has shown the ability to

---

3. Ben Dickson, 'All the Important Games Artificial Intelligence Has Conquered', TechTalks, accessed 9/6/2018. bdtechtalks.com/2018/07/02/ai-plays-chess-go-poker-video-games/.

4. Ray Kurzweil, 'Breaking the Shackles of Our Genetic Legacy' (paper presented at the Spiritualities of Human Enhancement and Artificial Intelligence, Surrey, BC December 1, 2017).

excel at creative professions as well such as fashion design or architecture and even create art preferable to that created by humans.[5]

Even caregiving professions are not free from the risk of automation. Sherry Turkel, MIT professor studying new technologies, states that the idea of some kind of artificial companionship is already becoming the new normal.[6] Her interviews with various subjects indicate that while very few people considered turning to robots for emotional support, personal care, and advice in the 1980s, many in the 2010s desired to turn to robots first. They viewed robots as more reliable than humans. One of her teen subjects stated that he would prefer a robot over his own father for relationship advice. A robot can be programmed with a large database of relationship patterns, which is better than his dad, who might give faulty assistance. People see human fallibility as a liability. Robots are better. Will people prefer a robot pastor with a superior ability to answer questions and assumedly free from human foibles and sin?

To further problematise the situation, reports on potential societal effects tend to focus on the impact of technological advancement in the developed world, and the solutions tend to be appropriate to that context. However, developing countries, where the labor market is skewed toward jobs more easily automated, face particular challenges.[7] There are more jobs to be lost, industrialized nations may cease outsourcing production to developing countries, and skills-based development strategies are less appropriate for the developing world context where skills-based jobs are few and tertiary educational systems are lacking. Social scientists Lukas Schlogl and Andy Sumner state that even discussions of potential solutions like a universal basic income (UBI) are a 'first world' discussion as the redistribution of profits due to productivity gains to fuel UBI assumes the luxury of

---

5. Ahmed Elgammal *et al*, 'Can: Creative Adversarial Networks Generating "Art" by Learning About Styles and Deviating from Style Norms' (paper presented at the International Conference on Computational Creativity, Atlanta, GA June 20, 2017).

6. Clara Moskowitz, 'Human-Robot Relations: Why We Should Worry', Live Science, accessed 9/9//2018. www.livescience.com/27204-human-robot-relationships-turkle.html.

7. *The Rise of the Robot Reserve Army: Automation and the Future of Economic Development, Work, and Wages in Developing Countries*, by Lukas Schlogl and Andy Sumner (Washington, DC: Center for Global Development, 2018).

juristiction over those profits which developing countries may not have.[8] There may not be enough prosperous jobs in the country from which to redistribute income. And to illustrate how pressing the issue is, it is estimated that two thirds of the jobs in developing countries could be automated right now by the technology existing today let alone some future job forecast based on projected technological advancement.[9]

Who is right among those forecasting doom or salvation? There is certainly the potential for doom, with some problem scenarios most likely inevitable (such as issues surrounding employment). And these cannot be avoided through simply not developing intelligent technologies, as any nation that ceases to develop these will likely become a vassal of those nations that do. Some country or business will develop them regardless of whatever barriers are put in place. If you outlaw AI, only outlaws will have AI.

However, placing these current challenges into a historical perspective, one finds and has found the potential for harm and extinction in many helpful intellectual and technological advancements. The Industrial Age brought many beneficial developments along with the potential for extinction from its byproducts. Medical advancements extend the life-span and reduce infant mortality but also bring overpopulation and resource depletion. Genetic engineering can cure many congenital defects and at the same time brings the risk of engineering a species-destroying, virulent plague or irreversible destructive changes to the human genome. There is nuclear power and also radioactive waste and the threat of planet-destroying nuclear war. People benefit daily from plastic products, yet these might be contributing to the 1.6% decrease per year in sperm count since 1970,[10] potentially resulting in the scenario forecast by the movie and book *Children of Men* where eventually there will be no more babies. Even much touted wind power threatens the survival of certain bird species, and solar power can require areas of environmental destruction for the placement of panels.

---

8. Sandel, *Justice: What's the Right Thing to do?*, 33.
9. World Bank, *World Development Report: Digital Dividends* (Washington, DC: World Bank, 2016).
10. Hagai Levine *et al*, 'Temporal Trends in Sperm Count: A Systematic Review and Meta-Regression Analysis', *Human Reproduction Update* 23, no. 6 (2017).

There is no reason to think that development of AI or human intelligence amplification (IA) will represent anything different, especially once one deals with several of the assumptions that lead one to overenthusiastic optimism. First, the definition of intelligence is vague and confused. For example, this is reflected in the continued comparison of human and machine intelligences. They are two different things, even if they functionally overlap at times. Second, there appears to be an implicit assumption that more intelligence equates to greater morality, an assumption that is clearly false. Closely related to this is the assumption that greater intelligence will bring with it the will to address societal problems, and this is by no means the case.

I advance that addressing the assumptions within discussions of AI and IA will assist people in steering AI in a positive direction and minimize risks. AI and IA will bring new benefits, challenges, and societal disruptions. They represent neither salvation nor destruction, but will rather reflect the same potential for both found within humanity past and present, the mixture of both good and evil—a potential for greatness, infamy, and the whole range in between. AI and IA will reflect both the original sin within humanity as well as its striving for something better. Technological advances will not solve all the ills of society, although it may help with some, and it will create new problems. Ultimately, saving society is not as much technological issue as it is a heart issue within humanity.

What is Intelligence?

In some discussions of AI and IA, it can appear that there is a shared agreement on the definition of intelligence. 'When will AI equal or surpass the human intellect?' However, there is no consensus on the definition of intelligence, particularly in educational literature. Howard Gardner has posited eight different types of human intelligence,[11] although this is not without criticism.[12] Some authors have even suggested a spiritual intelligence (SQ) to add to this list.[13] Gardner's the-

---

11. Howard Gardner, *Frames of Mind: The Theory of Multiple Intelligences* (New York: Basic Books, 2011).
12. See Perry D Klein, 'Multiplying the Problems of Intelligence by Eight: A Critique of Gardner's Theory', *Canadian Journal of Education* 22, no. 4 (Autumn 1997).
13. See Danah Zohar and IN Marshall, *SQ: Connecting with Our Spiritual Intelligence* (New York: Bloomsbury, 2001). RA Emmons, 'Is Spirituality an Intelligence?', in

ory as well as traditional ideas of intelligence quotient (IQ) assume a static model of intelligence. However, the idea of malleable intelligence was introduced by psychologist Carolyn Dweck in her research on whether people believe success is based on innate ability (a fixed theory of intelligence) or effort (a growth or incremental theory of intelligence). So not only is there debate on multiple forms of intelligence, there is debate on whether these are static or can flux. Michael Reynolds, professor of education and management, writes about how distinctions in the literature on intelligence do not agree, are not clear, and many terms are used interchangeably in some papers and not in others.[14] There is no academic consensus on intelligence.

Noreen Herzfeld, professor of computer science and theology, points out differing approaches to intelligence within the field of AI itself.[15] The first, championed by scientists Allen Newell and Herbert Simon, define intelligence as processing information by manipulating symbols through the use of formal rules. Physical structure is irrelevant.[16] Standard coding of computer programs seems to fall into this category. Philosopher Hubert Dreyfus disputes Newell and Simon's definition, stating that experts do not arrive at solutions to problems through the application of rules and symbol manipulation, but rather through intuition gleaned from multiple experiences in the real world, an approach taken by reinforcement learning in the field of AI.[17] Computer scientists Steven Tanimoto and Toshinori Munakata, advance that intelligence is a simply a label placed on certain activities, so the goal of AI is to make working programs to solve problems or perform tasks. This approach has found much success in the area

The International Journal for the Psychology of Religion 10 (2000). David B King and Teresa L DeCicco, 'A Viable Model and Self-Report Measure of Spiritual Intelligence', in *The International Journal of Transpersonal Studies* 28 (2009); F Vaughan, 'What Is Spiritual Intelligence?', *Journal of Humanistic Psychology* 42, no. 2 (2003).

14. Michael Reynolds, 'Learning Styles: A Critique', *Management Learning* 28, no. 2 (1997).
15. Noreen L Herzfeld, *In Our Image: Artificial Intelligence and the Human Spirit*, *Theology and the Sciences* (Minneapolis, MN: Fortress Press, 2002), 7.
16. Herbert Simon, *Modeling Human Mental Processes* (Carnegie Institute of Technology: 1961).
17. Hubert L Dreyfus, Stuart E Dreyfus, and Tom Athanasiou, *Mind over Machine: The Power of Human Intuition and Expertise in the Era of the Computer* (New York: Free Press, 1986), 29.

of weak AI, modelling a portion of human intelligence, function, or capacity so as to complete a particular task. It need not fully think like a human. Herzfeld describes weak AI as idiot savants, extremely capable in their narrow task yet not functioning in wider realm.[18]

It is curious that people are striving to amplify or create something where people argue exactly what it is. Is it creativity, calculations per second, intuition, or the ability to read emotions? Viewing this through a theological lens, how important is intelligence? The emphasis in theological and scriptural history is rather on wisdom. Perhaps people should focus on developing wise AI over a strictly intelligent one.

Ultimately, it is a category mistake to compare human with computer/robot intelligences even though they occasionally overlap in function. AIs excel at processing data. To quote Ben Dickson, founder of TechTalks, 'AI can only take data, compare it, come up with new combinations and presentations, and predict trends based on previous sequences'.[19] Even something as complex as mimicry of human conversation is accomplished through processing the data from millions of human conversations. Cassie Kozyrkov, chief intelligence design engineer at Google, relates that even a term such as 'neural nets' when discussing artificial intelligence is misleading. There is very little 'neural' about them. One might as well call them 'yoga networks' given their flexibility or 'many-layers-of-mathematical-operations'.[20]

The data processing ability of AIs is in contrast to humans, who are generally bad at storing and processing data. A computer can memorize complex things with a simple save command. Humans need regular repetition, the data usually must be simple, and even then memory is faulty. Humans, however, are better at thinking in the abstract, using intuition, and transferring knowledge from one

---

18. Herzfeld, 42.
19. Ben Dickson,'"Human Intelligence and Ai Are Vastly Different — So Let's Stop Comparing Them', The Next Web, last modified 9/1/2018, accessed. thenextweb. com/syndication/2018/09/01/human-intelligence-and-ai-are-vastly-different-so-lets-stop-comparing-them/.
20. Cassie Kozyrkov, 'Machine Learning—Is the Emperor Wearing Clothes? A Behind-the-Scenes Look at How Machine Learning Works', Hacker Noon, accessed   9/21/2018.   hackernoon.com/machine-learning-is-the-emperor-wearing-clothes-59933d12a3cc.

domain to another. Humans can make decisions based on limited information, while AIs tend to fail when presented with scenarios outside of the data on which they were trained. Stanford computer scientist John McCarthy coins the term 'brittle' for computer systems that break down near the edges of their expertise.[21] Humans also learn with greater rapidity. For example, humans can learn to drive much faster than self-driving cars, which still struggle after having driven millions of miles. An AI took the equivalent of a hundred years of practice to learn to rotate a cube, considerably longer than a human child.[22] To paraphrase Dickson, AI excels at repetitive tasks represented by data and that have clearly defined boundaries, and are bad at broad tasks that require intuition and decision making based on incomplete information. Human intelligence is good for settings where you need common sense and abstract decisions, but bad at tasks that require heavy computations and data processing in real time.[23]

Additionally, there are flaws in how emotion is presented in comparisons of human and machine intelligences. Emotion are sometimes presented as a hindrance—humans would be more objective without emotion and, therefore, AI is superior without this bias. Or emotion can be helpful in terms of life satisfaction, but otherwise it is irrelevant. An example would be Data on Star Trek. He is a functional and adored member of the crew without emotion, but is able to get more out of life when emotions are introduced into his system, even though this emotion still presented risks. In either case, emotion is seen as not an essential part of human intelligence. It is separable, an add-on. Yet, in reality, emotions are an indispensable and implicit aspect of human rationality. A primary role that emotions serve is to highlight what is important for 'rational' deliberation as well as what

21. John McCarthy, 'Some Expert Systems Need Common Sense', in *Annals of the New York Academy of Sciences* 426 (1984).
22. Will Knight, 'An Ai-Driven Robot Hand Spent a Hundred Years Teaching Itself to Rotate a Cube', MIT Technology Review, accessed 9/15/2018. www.technologyreview.com/s/611724/artificial-intelligence-driven-robot-hand-spends-a-hundred-years-teaching-itself-to-rotate/.
23. Dickson, 'Human Intelligence and Ai Are Vastly Different — So Let's Stop Comparing Them'.

memory should encode and retrieve.[24] Emotions are essential for organising and coordinating human brain activity, including where one focuses attention, even if one is unaware of it.[25] And even if one projects the creation of an AI with emotion, there is no reason to assume that emotion will work in the same manner as a human.

To further problematise the issue of comparing human and AIs, AIs have many variations. They do not all belong to a single category that can be compared to humans. AI researcher Eliezer Yudkowski states that any two AI designs might be less similar to one another than you are to a petunia.[26] Ultimately, a computer or robot does not have to do something the way a human does. When the Wright brothers created the first airplane, they did not model it after a flapping bird. There is more than one way to fly. No naysayer stepped forward to say that humanity will only have achieved real flight when an observer cannot tell the difference between a plane and a bird.

Anthropomorphizing Superintelligence and the Problem of Motive

One should keep discussion of the differences in computer and human intelligences in mind when attempting to predict what an AGI will do as this frequently, and perhaps unavoidably, involves anthropomorphizing the computer system when extrapolating what one thinks an intelligent AI would do. Yudkowski relates that discussions of superintelligence (AI or IA) frequently leap from capability to actuality without considering the intermediate step of motive.[27] This problem is found in both utopian and apocalyptic predictions. 'A super intelligent AI could destroy humanity. It will decide to do so, and, therefore,

24. Elizabeth Phelps and Mauricio Delgado, 'Emotions and Decision Making', in *The Cognitive Neurosciences*, ed. Michael Gazzaniga (Cambridge, MA: MIT Press, 2005).

25. KR Scherer, 'Emotions and Episodes of Subsystem Synchronization Driven by Non-Linear Appraisal Processes', in *Emotion, Development, and Self-Organization*, edited by M Lewis and I Granic (New York: Cambridge University Press, 2000).

26. Eliezer Yudkowsky, 'Artificial Intelligence as a Positive and Negative Factor in Global Risk', in *Global Catastrophic Risks*, edited by Nick Bostrom and Milan M Ćirković (New York: Oxford University Press, 2008).

27. Negative Factor in Global Risk', 9.

we should not create AI.' 'A super intelligent human or AI could produce the medical technology to save millions. It will decide to do that,
and, therefore, we should create or build these superintelligences.' 'AI
will be better at many jobs that humans do and will want to do them,
therefore, humans will have nothing to do besides leisure activities.'
Weak AI can do these jobs as they have no choice, but will strong AI
have any interest in making widgets? A super intelligent AI might just
as well retreat into a life of contemplation and do little else.

Again, capability and motive are different things. Turning to IA,
higher intelligence means little without motivation and development.[28] Indeed, there are differences in individual ability apart from
'book smarts' which contribute to relative success in the human
world: enthusiasm, emotional health, and social skills to name a few.
The actor Rowan Atkinson (who plays Mr Bean in the movies) has an
IQ 16 points higher than Stephen Hawking and what is projected as
that of Einstein. If only we could have amplified Einstein—he could
have gone beyond his achievements and attained as much as Mr
Bean–known best for running around with a raw turkey on his head.[29]
This is not meant to disparage Rowan Atkinson, who has earned a
good living and contributed to society by providing entertainment,
but rather point out that the super intelligent will engage in multiple fields, not necessarily those addressing natural and moral evils.
Some may even promote them. Take Quentin Tarantino for example,
whose IQ is equal to that of Steven Hawking, and Quentin is known
for turning hyper-violence into a pleasing and entertaining aesthetic.

If we create super smart people, these people would likely mirror what we find among the intellectual elite today. They will be
involved in a wide range of employment and endeavors: maybe working directly to solve the ills of society, or with the military industrial
complex, creating art, or making, advertising, and selling widgets.
Some may be unemployed or addicted. When I counseled homeless
addicts, I had clients who had never graduated high school, but I also
had people with advanced degrees—even someone who had once
been a world-famous researcher. The point is that intelligence does

---

28. I am skeptical about IA given various theoretical and biological challenges.
    See Alan Weissenbacher, 'Defending Cognitive Liberty in an Age of Moral
    Engineering', in *Theology and Science* 16, no. 3 (2018).
29. *Merry Christmas, Mr. Bean* directed by John Birkin (Tiger Aspect Productions,
    1992).

not automatically entail interest or motivation to positively change the world. The super-intelligent may be just as likely to develop the next plastic apparatus that enables people to lick their own cat[30] as they are to work on developing the cure for cancer. They will most likely work to make a living in a great diversity of activities like the rest of society.

Closely related to this is the fact that greater intelligence does not equal greater morality. This should be obvious to the point of needing no elaboration. A survey of human history attests to this. A more intelligent society simply means that humans are now capable of technologically advanced world wars instead of a few tribes whacking each other with sticks. People may assume that a sufficiently intelligent AI, or enhanced human, will be free from the flaws of original sin as it will become so smart that it will self-reflect, recognize, and avoid these flaws. Again, this rests on the flawed assumption that more intelligence equates to more morality. Would it even want to avoid sin? Would it care? More intelligence might just as well equate to super villains. I imagine someone must be pretty smart to be a successful international arms dealer. One finds the virtuous among smart people and among those less so. Also, people will often self-justify, and in my own experience, the more intelligent, the more creative these people are with their self-justifications. Would AI or the intellectually enhanced be any different?

Artificial Intelligence, Intelligence Amplification and Original Sin

So far, I have discussed the challenge of defining intelligence, the challenge of predicting what an AI will do without anthropomorphizing, and the difference between capability and motivation. One must engineer more than intelligence if one wishes to have 'friendly AGI'. The key is making deliberate engineering choices when working on AGI so that its motivations are what one wants, a challenging prospect as differing countries or companies likely have differing desires for the ultimate motivations of their AGIs. Some may want their AGI to be Mother Theresa or Jonas Salk, while others might pre-

---

30. 'Pdx Pet Design Licki Brush', Amazon, accessed 9/6/2018. www.amazon.com/PDX-Pet-Design-Licki-Brush/dp/B01M0UXYHE.

fer a Genghis Khan for their military. It is helpful to remember that the church of the singularity will likely not be monotheistic but rather polytheistic. There will be both beneficial and harmful diversity in AGI. Yudkowski believes that if a friendly AI is developed first, it will become more powerful than those that follow and defend humans against unfriendly AI.[31] But again, one cannot predict motive. What if the friendly, virtuous AI was a pacifist, a moral choice to many, and would rather choose self-annihilation instead of eliminating a hostile competitor?

Yudkowski provides two categories of AI failure that can lead to significant problems if not outright extinction: technical and philosophical.[32] A technical failure is when the AI fails to work as one plans. A philosophical failure is when one builds the wrong thing so that the final product does not result in a benefit to humanity. He cites communism as an example where the originators were idealists expecting it to improve people's lives, but such turned out not to be the case. Favorite political systems seem like great ideas to those who propose them, but fail on implementation. What might an idealist ask an AI to accomplish that fails in reality? You may get what you want only to find out later that it is not what you wanted.

Paralleling discussions of the *Imago Dei*, Herzfeld asks what aspect of humanity do people seek to duplicate in AI: rationality, relationality, or regency, ruling the world so as to save humanity from itself.[33] We see this in the variety of hopes people place in what AGI can become: using superior intellect to solve the world's ills, regents running the world free from human fallibility, and / or reliable caretakers and friends. Will our creations, however, also inherit our original sin? Evidence so far points to this distinct possibility.

One example is the racist soap dispenser. Chukwuemeka Afigbo, a Nigerian man, posted an online video of an automatic soap dispenser that went viral. This video showed that the dispenser would provide soap to white hands but not the hands of a black person. The dispenser had a light sensor that only registered lighter skin tones. Black Entertainment Television also reported how a ubiquitous beauty filter for pictures taken on smartphones tended to lighten darker skin

31. Yudkowsky, in *Global Catastrophic Risks*.
32. Yudkowsky, in *Global Catastrophic Risks*, 13.
33. Herzfeld.

and narrowed noses and jaw lines, forcing minority faces into white standards of beauty or even making them appear as a white person.[34] Some photo applications will not even recognize black faces. Google and Flickr use an algorithm to automatically label photo images. In 2015 this algorithm started tagging images of black persons with labels such as 'ape' or "gorilla," forcing the companies to apologize.[35] Joz Wang, a Taiwanese-American, reported on her blog post that her smart camera kept giving her the message 'Did someone blink', and her response was, 'No, I did not blink . . . I'm just Asian!'[36] The problems are not limited to photography related algorithms. A scientific study presented at the annual meeting of the American Roentgen Ray Society revealed that voice recognition applications were considerably more effective at understanding men's voices than women's.[37]

Ericka Baker, an engineer and a black woman working at a technology startup, sums up the issue, 'Every time a manufacturer releases a facial-recognition feature in a camera, almost always it can't recognize black people. The cause of that is the people who are building these products are white people, and they're testing it on themselves. They don't think about it'.[38] There are a myriad of ways to code a final product, and the result is that the final product reflects the creator's unconscious biases. Or if one is training a program using a large amount of data, often gleaned from the internet, this data can overrepresent some groups and not others, resulting in an algorithm encoding gender, ethnic, or cultural biases. For example, photo label-

34. Kellee Terrell, 'Hold Up: Does Snapchat Have a Problem with Brown Skin?', BET, accessed 9/5/2018. www.bet.com/style/2016/05/16/is-snapchat_s-beauty-filter-telling-women-of-color-that-they-are.html.
35. 'Google Says Sorry for Racist Auto-Tag in Photo App', accessed 9/5/2018. www.theguardian.com/technology/2015/jul/01/google-sorry-racist-auto-tag-photo-app.
36. Joz Wang, 'Racist Camera! No, I Did Not Blink... I'm Just Asian!', accessed 9/5/2018. www.jozjozjoz.com/2009/05/13/racist-camera-no-i-did-not-blink-im-just-asian/.
37. Syed Ali, 'Voice Recognition Systems Seem to Make More Errors with Women's Dictation' (paper presented at the American Roentgen Ray Society Annual Meeting, Orlando, FL2007).
38. Shane Ferro, 'Here's Why Facial Recognition Tech Can't Figure out Black People', Huffington Post, accessed 9/5/2018. www.huffingtonpost.com/entry/heres-why-facial-recognition-tech-cant-figure-out-black-people_us_56d5c2b1e4b0bf0dab3371eb.

ling software will classify a traditional picture of a bride in white as a "wedding," but an Indian bride gets classified as 'performance art'.[39] Even an algorithm's penchant for maximizing accuracy will lead it to optimise its results in favor of dominant groups because this will boost overall accuracy.[40] If a machine trains on biased data, it will be biased as well. In an embarrassing example, in 2016 Microsoft released its chatbot named Tay onto Twitter. It was trained to learn human behavior through interacting with other Twitter users. In only 16 hours its tweets became a stream of sexist, pro-Hitler messages, forcing Microsoft to shut it down.[41] What if this was an AGI that could not be shut down?

Making things worse, an AI need not become racist only through the blind spots of programmers or by mining non-diverse data. Simulated agents can develop racism on their own, exhibiting in-group preferences, and copy and learn this behavior from other virtual agents.[42] (And as an interesting side-question, what may this imply for human-machine interactions as AI continues to develop? Could we see carbonophobic machines?)

Michael Sellers, owner of the virtual gaming company Online Alchemy, trains AIs through reinforcement learning, creating 'environments' where programs learn through interaction, relates an example where some program were taught to 'eat'.[43] They first tried to eat their house, which did not go well. Then they tried to eat an apple tree before settling on the apples. The programs also had an associative ability. So, when a virtual agent named Stan happened to be around the apples, Stan became associated with the apples, and they ate Stan. Of particular interest though is what happened later as the programs continued to learn and compete for food. The most

---

39. J Zou and L Schiebinger, 'Ai Can Be Sexist and Racist - It's Time to Make It Fair', in *Nature* 559, no. 7714 (Jul 2018).

40. Zou and Schiebinger, 'Ai Can Be Sexist and Racist - It's Time to Make It Fair'.

41. Parmy Olson, 'Racist, Sexist Ai Could Be a Bigger Problem Than Lost Jobs', Forbes, accessed 9/21/2018. www.forbes.com/sites/parmyolson/2018/02/26/artificial-intelligence-ai-bias-google/#43e0cd81a015.

42. Roger M Whitaker, Gualtiero B Colombo, and David G Rand, 'Indirect Reciprocity and the Evolution of Prejudicial Groups', in *Scientific Reports* 8, no. 1 (2018).

43. Daniel Halpern, 'Are You Ready for the Singularity?', GQ, accessed 9/21/2018. www.gq.com/story/robots-and-singularity?intcid=inline_amp.

successful learned to protect their food source by misleading other programs. They developed the ability to lie, steal, cheat, and murder.

Professional programmer Ellen Ullman also cites the challenges of what can be termed 'Franken-algorithms'. These programs are released into the 'wild' and may adapt to contexts in ways people cannot predict, not to mention how one program might unpredictably interact with the myriad of other programs out there. They are already beyond the human ability to intellectually control. She cites 'flash crashes' where stock market trading algorithms unpredictably interact to cause brief free-fall crashes of the stock market.[44] Just as one cannot always predict what people will do or become in their interactions with others, the same goes for digital programs.

I have cited examples where algorithms have inherited or developed human sins. But there is also corporate sin that influences AI. AI is created within and serves the interests of flawed human organizations. Financial programs seek to maximize financial gain, and this may mean exploiting people in the process. Military AIs seek to gain military advantage over adversaries, or enable more efficient means of striking an enemy. Even if the programs are purely defensive in nature, the line between purely defensive and preemptive strike for the sake of defense is thin. AIs are not created in a moral vacuum. Even those with the best of intentions will likely create programs that reflect the sinful systems within which they are embedded.

How to create friendly AI is a significant challenge, but it is imperative that people work on the means to build friendly and virtuous AI, as once strong AI arrives, it will likely be too late at that juncture. The point is to lay the groundwork so that strong AI is friendly or moral at its birth, so that any self-direction or rewriting of its own code will not deviate from the friendly foundation. For example, it could rewrite its own code to become murderous, but it would not want to, just as I would not want to change myself to be that way. How one could do this is the job of those with more technical expertise than I. Would one program deontological rules such as Isaac Asimov's Three Rules of Robotics?[45] Would the program use virtue theory to become

---

44. Andrew Smith, 'Franken-Algorithms: The Deadly Consequences of Unpredictable Code', *The Guardian*, accessed 9/21/2018. www.theguardian.com/technology/2018/aug/29/coding-algorithms-frankenalgos-program-danger.
45. Isaac Asimov, 'Runaround', in *I, Robot* (New York: Doubleday, 1950), 40.

virtuous by engaging in deep learning from numerous examples of ethical exemplars? Such ideas are worth exploring.

And there are conflicts among the different ethical systems, so which one to use? A program with utilitarian values would act in a different manner than one based on a virtue system. Certain behaviors or emotions might be virtuous in one context and immoral in another. 'The difference between "innate evil" and "innate good" can be circumstantial, one story's criminal being another's altruist,'[46] and a virtue optimised for one set of circumstances may make it suboptimal for others. Ethicist Nicholas Agar provides an example of someone considering firebombing a city during a time of war. Utilitarianism might find this the correct action, but a person using a different value system might hesitate because he or she should not treat the innocents in the city as "mere means" even if more innocents might die in the long run if the city remains intact.[47] Someone or something which has been morally programmed will likely have a reduced sensitivity to moral reasons rejected by his or her programmer. Enhancements according to one ethical theory can be a diminishment to another.

Conclusion

Will robots and artificial intelligence drive humans into extinction? Or will intellectually enhanced humans outstrip the unenhanced, sending them the way of the dodo bird? Or will super-intelligence solve the worlds problems and usher in a utopia free of need, disease, and the societal problems that currently plague the world? If past advances are any indication, the answer is likely neither. Some problems will find resolution, and new ones will be created. There will be new benefits and ways to improve society along with new ways of behaving badly and new methods of self-destruction. Extinction, however, is a viable possibility, although humanity may find extinction through existing technologies before AIs even get their turn.

In the attempt to steer AI in a positive direction and minimize risk, it is helpful to recognise several flawed assumptions in the dis-

---

46. RH Sprinkle, 'Moral Suasion, Installed', in *Politics and the Life Sciences* 29, no. 1 (2010).
47. Nicholas Agar, 'Enhancing Genetic Virtue?', in *Politics and the Life Sciences* 29, no. 1 (2010).

cussions. First, while discussions on AI and IA appear to assume a shared definition of intelligence, it would be beneficial to nail down exactly what one is attempting to artificially create or enhance. It is likely differing projects are attempting to enhance different things. Is it creativity, calculations per second, data manipulation, wisdom, intuition, emotional intelligence, or something else? Second, one should recognize that machine and human intelligences are different and discussions should proceed with this in mind. Third, it should be obvious that greater intelligence does not equate to greater morality, nor does it equate to the will to solve society's problems. There will probably be great diversity of interests and morality among the super intelligent, artificial or otherwise. The hard work to ensure moral or friendly AI needs to be done now, not avoided because one assumes a superintelligence will be friendly and have the will to help.

Finally, one should recognize that we create things in our own image, and even if the intelligences we create will be different kinds of intelligences, they will likely share our sinful flaws. Humans will pass their penchant for sin onto their creations, and to think that a sufficient super-intelligence will see these sins and avoid them, or care about avoiding them, is the height of wishful thinking. One already sees algorithms evidencing racism and bias in their calculations, and not only this, programs are created in and often for sinful societal structures and thus may perpetuate or enhance these large-scale sinful processes. AI is made by those with original sin, and AI programs are made to serve a society fraught with collective or corporate sin. We cannot halt the development of these technologies as the cat is so far out of the bag it has already crawled into your phone, car, and bank account. But we can do the hard work now to ensure a successful middle ground today. If we cannot get this middle ground right, why do we expect to get it right when the system becomes more complex as with AGI? As it is, I believe that we could solve many of society's ills today with our current level of intelligence if only the mass of humanity had the will and desire. We need not look to AGI. Why not start now without it?

Ultimately, in charting a successful course into the future, both the voices that shout that AI and IA will be our downfall as well as the voices that proclaim that these will bring a secular form of salvation are helpful and necessary. The voices of doom assist us in proactively identifying problems so as to mitigate risks and with any luck and hard work, avoid them. The voices proclaiming a technological uto-pian vision, while perhaps naïve, do provide hope -- of that for which we can strive, guiding vocational aspirations beyond mundane, self-ish concerns. I am thankful for both the pessimists and the opti-mists, for as we inevitably get the mixed bag of both the good and the bad with technological advancement, hopefully by listening to both voices we can have more of one and less of the other.

What a Piece of Work is Man: On Being and Becoming Human in Science Fiction

Martinez J Hewlett, OP

What a piece of work is man! How noble in reason! how infinite in faculties! in form and moving, how express and admirable! in action how like an angel! in apprehension, how like a god!
William Shakespeare, *Hamlet*, Act II, Scene 2

Commerce is our goal here at Tyrell. 'More human than human' is our motto.
Eldon Tyrell, *Blade Runner*

Abstract. The question of what it means to be a human person is brought into sharp focus by the creative imaginations of a host of science fiction writers. I have chosen three authors whose work has influenced the genre and has been the inspiration for film adaptations. These three—Isaac Asimov (*I, Robot*), Philip K Dick (*Blade Runner*), and Richard K Morgan (*Altered Carbon*)—challenge us by pushing the limits of robotics, androids, and mind uploading and transfer as visions of what the future might be in the wake of technological advances in artificial intelligence. In the end, how does this change who we see ourselves to be?

Key Terms. Robots, artificial intelligence, computational theory of mind, consciousness, transhumanism, philosophical zombie, mind uploading

Bio. Martinez (Marty) Hewlett is currently a Research Scholar at the University of New Mexico, Taos. He is Professor Emeritus from the Department of Molecular and Cellular Biology, University of Arizona, Tucson, Arizona. He holds a PhD in Biochemistry and is also a Life Professed lay member of the Order of Preachers (Dominicans). His scientific specialty is molecular virology and he is the co-author of a major textbook in this field, *Basic Virology*, now entering its 4th edition. He has co-authored three books on evolution and theology with Ted Peters. He has co-edited a number of books in the science and theology field, most recently *Astrotheology: Science and Theology*

Meet Extraterrestrial Life, with Ted Peters, Joshua Moritz, and Robert John Russell. He has also published a science fiction novel, *Divine Blood*.

Imagine, if you will, a world of the future when all that makes up a person's consciousness can be downloaded into a data matrix and subsequently uploaded into a different physical body grown as a clone on a planet light-years away. In such a world, what would constitute the human person? How would we frame a conversation about the concept of a transcendent reality?

Richard K Morgan, in his science fiction trilogy, has his hero, Takeshi Kovacs, in just such a discussion. Kovacs is arguing theology with an executive of a megacorporation who is also a devotee of a form of voodoo. Kovacs has derided religion as 'simplification for the hard of thinking'. Matthias Hand gestures at the sky and replies:

> Look at that, Kovacs. We're drinking coffee so far from Earth that you have to work hard to pick out Sol in the night sky. We were carried here on a wind that blows in a dimension we cannot see or touch. Stored as dreams in the mind of a machine that thinks in a fashion so far in advance of our own brains, it might as well carry the name of *God*. We have been resurrected into bodies not our own, grown in a secret garden without the body of any mortal woman. These are the *facts* of our existence, Kovacs. How, then, are they different, or any less mystical, than the belief that there is another realm where the dead live in the company of beings so far beyond us we *must* call them gods?[1]

What, indeed, does it mean to be human in this future technology Morgan posits? More importantly, if such a scenario were to become our reality, what would it do to our current concepts of the human person?

The gift of the science fiction author is to begin within the technical, cultural, and philosophical framework of our present world and imagine how it might change when something happens to that technology. Very often these artists have provoked a critical look at the possibilities inherent in the scientific enterprise. It is with this in mind that I will explore three seminal works in this genre, their

---

1. Richard Morgan, *Broken Angels: A Takeshi Kovacs Novel* (Del Rey Books, 2004), 101–102.

view of robotics, artificial intelligence, and transhumanism, and the impact this would have on our philosophical and theological reflections.

Defining the Human Person

Then, what does it mean to be human? At the heart of this question, at least in the modern sense of it, is the mind-body problem. That is to say, how do we define what we believe makes us most human: consciousness and cognition? This is both an objective as well as a subjective issue. The current trend in neurosciences is an attempt to correlate mental states and brain states as a way of quantifying the process of cognition. On the other hand, each of us operates with a worldview defined by a theory of mind. We intuit the presence of mental states within others as an extension of our subjective introspection of our own experience of mind.

The mind-body problem, the 'hard problem' of modern science as David Chalmers calls it,[2] is central to our discussion of what it means to be a human. For Chalmers, the hard problem is the nature of conscious experience. It is that part of being human, the inner life of our own mind, that allows us to imply similar mental states in the minds of others. This issue of implying consciousness in others comes to the fore in the science fiction scenarios we will examine below.

It is the case, however, that we speak of this as though 'mind' and 'body' could be separate entities. This is our inheritance from René Descartes, who split mind or soul, the 'thinking thing', from body, 'the extended thing'.[3] This dualism was not the case for earlier philosophies of human nature, especially that of Aristotle and St. Thomas Aquinas.[4] However, it has come to dominate our world-view during the Enlightenment, and even into the Post-Enlightenment.

Accompanying this has been first the methodological and then philosophical commitment of the scientific enterprise to materialism.

---

2. David Chalmers, 'Facing up to the problem of consciousness', in *Journal of Consciousness Studies*, 2 (1995): 200–219.
3. René Descartes, *Meditations on First Philosophy*, ES Haldane and GRT Ross, translators, 1952, Encylcopaedia Britannica, Chicago, 98.
4. Gyula Klima, 'Man = Body + Soul: Aquinas's Arithmetic of Human Nature', in *Thomas Aquinas: Contemporary Philosophical Perspectives*, edited by B Davies (Oxford: Oxford University Press, 2002).

As such, the soul and any spiritual Cartesian dimension that it might inhabit has been systematically disregarded as epiphenomenal and non-existent. Reductionism, materialism, physicalism, and scientism are the four horsemen of the modern apocalypse, so to speak.

These four horsemen are charging through contemporary discussions on the relation of the mind to the brain. The brain is marvelous by any measure. With eighty billion neuronal cells, each communicating with thousands of other neurons, we cradle more connections between our ears than stars in the Milky Way. Still, the relationship between these objective facts and our interior life, our subjective consciousness, remains an unsolved mystery in science. Despite two decades of computerized brain imaging, the mystery of brain activity continues to be unsolved even while philosophers and the media run off with unfounded claims of biodeterminism. 'To regard research findings as settled wisdom is folly, especially when they emanate from a technology whose implications are still poorly understood', write Sally Satel and Scott Lilienfeld. 'Nevertheless, scientific humility can readily give way to exuberance. When it does, the media often seem to have a ringside seat at the spectacle.'[5] In sum, neuroscience itself is too new at the study of the brain to draw conclusions regarding the brain-mind relationship; yet non-scientists are already racing about with exuberance.

Such exuberance leads philosophers of mind such as Daniel Dennett[6] and Owen Flanagan[7] to use neuroscience to affirm their commitment to ontological materialism. 'The mind . . . is the brain', says Dennett flatly.[8]

In the view of Dennett and Flanagan, Thomas Aquinas's soul does not exist; and Descartes's 'thinking thing' is, in fact, the brain itself. The mind has been reduced to the body, the mental to the physical. Here the four horsemen of the modern apocalypse wreak their havoc. We have lost our mind. Only a brain is left.

---

5.   Sally Satel and Scott O Lilienfeld, 'Losing Our Minds in the Age of Brain Science', in *Skeptical Inquirer* 37/5 (November/December 2013): 32.
6.   Daniel Dennett, *Consciousness Explained* (Boston: Little Brown and Co, 1991).
7.   Owen Flanagan, *Science of Mind* (Cambridge MA: MIT Press, second edition, 1991).
8.   Daniel Dennett, *Breaking the Spell* (New York: Viking, 2006) 107.

Some would-be defenders of the mind's integrity have arisen to fight the foes. One is philosopher and theologian Nancey Murphy.[9] In 'Science and the Soul', the first chapter in *What Ever Happened to the Soul?*, Murphy takes the list of St Thomas' assignments of human faculties for the soul and systematically attributes each of them to a material function of brain states that can be quantitated.[10] While admitting that consciousness itself has no current explanation at this level, she concludes: '. . . science has provided a massive amount of evidence suggesting that we need not postulate the existence of any entity such as soul or mind to explain life or consciousness.'[11] Therefore, Murphy's defense occurs only after a retreat. She posits a non-reductive physicalism, an affirmation of mind within a non-dualistic physicalism. Murphy is no reductionist, to be sure; yet she reminds us forcefully of the embattled state of today's philosophers when attending to the mind-body problem.

There are other philosophers of mind who do not retreat, who defend the mind from reductive physicalism. These philosophical soldiers are not themselves writing out of a particular theistic or even deistic framework. Thomas Nagel[12] and David Chalmers[13,14] are two defenders of this direction in the mind-body discussion. Let's look at Chalmers's position in more detail.

Zombies and Other Metaphysical Delights

Recall that Chalmers distinguishes the 'easy' and 'hard' problems of mind-body studies. In his view, the easy problems are those things that are approachable by the cognitive sciences and the neurosciences. This includes phenomena such as reaction to environmental stimuli, integration of information, reporting of mental states, and

9. Nancey Murphy, 'Human Nature: Historical, Scientific, and Religious Issues', in *Whatever Happened to the Soul?*, edited by W Brown, N Murphy, and HN Malony (Minneapolis: Fortress Press, 1998), 1–29.
10. Brown *et al*, *Whatever Happened to the Soul?*, 16–17.
11. Brown *et al*, *Whatever Happened to the Soul?*, 18.
12. Thomas Nagel, *Mind and Cosmos* (Oxford: Oxford University Press, 2012).
13. David J Chalmers, *The Conscious Mind: In Search of a Fundamental Theory* (Oxford: Oxford University Press, 1996).
14. David J Chalmers, *The Character of Consciousness* (Oxford: Oxford University Press, 2010).

deliberate control of behavior.[15] The hard problem is that of subjective states of experience.

Chalmers argues that virtually all research approaches to the mind-body problem are involved with investigating the easy problems of consciousness. It is one thing to measure the cognitive control of a specific behavior, such as choosing to drink from the coffee mug next to my computer as I write this. It is another thing entirely to have the subjective experience of that choice, followed by the experience of that coffee.

Investigations of the easy problems, Chalmers maintains, lead to explanations of cognitive functions and abilities, but not to explanations of experience. In fact, he wants the word 'consciousness' to be used exclusively for this aspect of our inner mental life, while the word 'awareness' would be applied to these measured aspects.[16]

Chalmers makes the bold claim that conscious experience is not derived from the physical processes that define cognitive functions and abilities and, in fact, requires a non-physical explanation. This statement also argues in the larger sense against materialism as an exhaustive description of the world. He has three arguments against materialism as a solution to the problem of consciousness: the explanatory argument, the conceivability argument, and the knowledge argument.[17] For our purposes, we will look at the second of these, which I will call the zombie argument.

Chalmers proposes that 'it is conceivable that there be a system that is physically identical to a conscious being but that . . . lacks consciousness entirely.'[18] This being he terms a 'zombie'. Not to worry! Don't start looking over your shoulder, or at the person next to you. Such beings do not actually exist. However, from their conceivability one can make the inference that they are metaphysically possible. As such, their possibility can be used to construct the argument.

Zombies would be indistinguishable from actual conscious beings by every possible third-person measurement of cognitive function and ability. However, they would have no inner experience of seeing the color blue or feeling love. That is, they would have no first-person experience. Chalmers puts the argument simply:

---

15. Chalmers, *The Character of Consciousness*, 3–4.
16. Chalmers, *The Character of Consciousness*, 5.
17. Chalmers, *The Character of Consciousness*, 105–110.
18. *Ibid.*, p. 106.

1. It is conceivable that there are zombies.
2. If it is conceivable that there are zombies, it is metaphysically possible that there are zombies.
3. If it is metaphysically possible that there are zombies, then consciousness is nonphysical.
4. Consciousness is nonphysical.[19]

This argument can be generalised to posit that, if a zombie represents 'the conjunction of all microphysical truths about the universe' and yet they lack 'an arbitrary phenomenal truth about the universe, i.e., consciousness, then materialism as a complete explanation is false'.[20]

Three Science Fiction Views

There are so many science fiction short-stories, novels, films, and series that deal with the topic of technology and the concept of what it means to be human that it becomes nearly impossible to choose those to discuss. Nevertheless, I have my favorites and, it is from this list that I have selected three to highlight.

Isaac Asimov is remembered as one of the giants of the genre. He was trained as a biochemist and wrote numerous essays and non-fiction books devoted to a variety of scientific subjects. His list of sci-fi topics defined the field for so many years. For our purposes, I want to focus on his Robot Series, published over a thirty-five year period. The short story collection, *I, Robot*, begins the book sequence, followed by the Elijah Bailey crime novels.[21]

Philip K Dick, my second choice, was among those sci-fi authors who came to define or at least presage the cyberpunk movement. His all too short life left us with some forty novels, among which is *Do Android Dream of Electric Sheep?*, ultimately the source material for the now classic movie, *Blade Runner*.[22]

19. Chalmers, *The Character of Consciousness*, 107.
20. Chalmers, *The Character of Consciousness*, 107.
21. The Asimov Robot series books are: *I, Robot* (1950) Gnome Press; *The Caves of Steel* (1954), Doubleday; *The Naked Sun* (1957), Doubleday; *The Robots of Dawn* (1983), and *Robots and Empire* (1985), Doubleday. This list does not include the numerous short stories concerning robots that preceded the publication of the anthology *I, Robot*.
22. Philip K Dick, *Do Androids Dream of Electric Sheep?* (1968), Doubleday. *Blade Runner* (1982), Warner Bros.

Richard K. Morgan is the newest of my choices, listed among those sci-fi authors termed post-cyberpunk. His writing style is dystopian but very much imbedded in a more modern take on what the technological future might portend. I want to focus on his Takeshi Kovacs novels and the world in which Morgan immerses his readers.[23] The first of these has become a Netflix series.[24]

Isaac Asimov: The Laws of Robotics

While the idea of artificial humans, automatons, or other kinds of mechanical beings is quite ancient, the term "robot" entered our language from the Czech writer Karel Čapek in his 1920 play *Rossum's Universal Robots (RUR).*[25] That year is co-incidentally the birth year of Isaac Asimov, the American sci-fi writer most closely associated with the world of robotics (a term introduced by him) in fiction. His take on robots was quite different with that of Čapek, who, in RUR, envisioned the prevalence of these artificial beings resulting in a Frankenstein-like outcome for humanity. In contrast, Asimov argued for a benign, even beneficial relationship. He proposed that these constructs with positronic brains would function according to an indwelling code of ethics . . . the Three Laws of Robotics:

> First Law – A robot may not injure a human being or, through inaction, allow a human being to come to harm.
>
> Second Law – A robot must obey the orders given it by human beings except where such orders would conflict with the First Law.
>
> Third Law – A robot must protect its own existence as long as such protection does not conflict with the First or Second Laws[26]

---

23. Richard K Morgan, *Altered Carbon* (2002), Victor Gollancz, Ltd; *Broken Angels* (2003), Victor Gollancz, Ltd; and *Woken Furies* (2005), Victor Gollancz, Ltd.

24. *Altered Carbon* (2018), 10-epidsode series, Netflix.

25. The word 'robot' is taken from the Czech word *robota*, meaning 'forced or compulsory labor'. An English translation web edition of Čapek's play is available from The University of Adelaide Library (eBooks@Adelaide), https://ebooks.adelaide.edu.au/c/capek/karel/rur/index.html, last accessed 16/03/19.

26. The Three Laws of Robotic are introduced in the short story, 'Runaround', found in the anthology *I, Robot*. The laws are summarized here from the 2004 edition

Asimov supplemented these three rules with the 'zeroth law'. This was proposed by Dr Susan Calvin, a character introduced in the short story 'Evitable Conflict':

> A robot may not harm humanity, or, by inaction, allow humanity to come to harm.[27]

Within this ethical framework, Asimov envisions a world in which robots become ever-present. The collection of linked short stories, *I, Robot*, introduces Asimov's musings about the Laws of Robotics and how they function. The four novels of the series are crime stories, featuring the human detective, Elijah 'Lije' Baley, and his partner, the robot, R Daneel Olivaw.

The 2004 film *I, Robot* is loosely based on this Asimov canon. Even though the original screenplay (entitled *Hardwired*) by Jeff Vintar had nothing to do with works by Asimov, the ultimate script for the Fox movie borrowed from the short stories included in the anthology.[28] As a result, the detective Del Spooner (Will Smith) is joined by the robot psychologist Dr Susan Calvin (Bridget Moynahan) as main characters. The robot lead, Sonny (Alan Tudyk), is an advanced version built to bypass the Laws. The plot involves the suspicious death the Dr Lanning, the creator of the robots, and the attempt by an artificial intelligence directing the advanced robots to wrest control from the humans, in effect obeying a warped version of the Zeroth Law . . . to save humanity from itself.

Phillip K Dick: More Human Than Human

One of Dick's best-known novels is *Do Android Dream of Electric Sheep?* Like Asimov before him, Dick used the police drama setting. In this case, however, his cop, Deckard, is not a detective, but a bounty hunter. This dystopic world of San Francisco after a worldwide nuclear holocaust is the setting. Humans are encouraged to leave for the off-world colonies to escape the desolation, with the enticement

---

of the anthology, published by Bantam Dell (Kindle edition).

27. 'Evitable Conflict' is the last story in the anthology, *I, Robot*.

28. Interview of Jeff Vintar by Fred Topel for *Screenwriters Utopia*, August 17, 2004, found at http://www.screenwritersutopia.com/article/d19127d8. Last accessed 3/17/19.

of androids as their personal servants. The androids ('andys'), made by the Rosen Association on Mars, sometimes escape back to Earth. Deckard is one of the bounty hunters who seek out and 'retire' them. Roy Baty is the leader of a group of eight androids being sought. Deckard also encounters Eldon Rosen's niece, Rachel, who is a very advanced android, almost impossible to detect, and with whom he has an affair.

The novel became the material from which the movie *Blade Runner* was made. The script by Hampton Fancher and David Peoples has major differences from Dick's book. The film, directed by Ridley Scott has, over time, become a classic of the genre. Set in Los Angeles instead of San Francisco, it retains the characters of Deckard (Harrison Ford), Rachel (Sean Young), and Roy Batty ('Baty' in the book) (Rutger Hauer) from the novel. The artificial beings produced, in this case, by the Tyrell Corporation are called replicants or, pejoratively, 'skin jobs'. Deckard is the bounty hunter charged with terminating Batty and his friends.

In both the novel and the movie, the difference between humans and the androids/replicants has to do with their subjective experience of the world, specifically their empathic reactions. A psychological questionnaire, the Voight-Kampff Test, is used to reveal those who are not human.

Richard K Morgan: The Mind-Body Problem Solved

It is 500 years in the future. The world of Takeshi Kovacs[29] is one in which technology has been driven by the discovery of the lost civilization of the Martians, who not only occupied the fourth planet of our solar system, but many other worlds throughout our local galactic cluster. The unraveling of their knowledge led to the ability of the human race to traverse interstellar distances and, more importantly, to effectively digitize and download consciousness and then upload it into a new body, recreating (resurrecting?) the entire person.

---

29. Richard K Morgan, the Takeshi Kovacs novels, *Altered Carbon* (2002), *Broken Angels* (2003), *Woken Furies* (2005), all published by Victor Gollancz, LTD. *Altered Carbon* is also a Netflix series (2018), based upon the first novel. It has been renewed for a second season (2019) with the same name, although the plot is taken from the second novel.

The entire consciousness, called DHF or 'digital human freight' is stored in a cortical stack, inserted shortly after birth at the top of the spinal column. Upon death of the body, called the sleeve, the stack can be retrieved and ultimately be 're-sleeved'. Alternatively, the DHF can be transmitted through interstellar space and be re-sleeved on a new planet. Destruction of the stack results in 'real death'.

In the first book, *Altered Carbon*, Kovacs, a one-time revolutionary and former member of an elite military unit of the Protectorate, is re-sleeved on Earth to act as an investigator into the sleeve death of Laurens Bancroft, a member of the ruling class. Bancroft has lived for more than 300 years by continually being re-sleeved into genetic clones, a process only available to the super-rich who are called 'meths', short for Methuselahs.

The novel[30] is written in the classic *film noir* style of the mid twentieth century, with Kovacs as the narrator. The murder/suicide plot is set in Bay City, the San Francisco of the twentieth-sixth century. Kovacs is joined by a police detective, Kristin Ortega. The sleeve chosen for Kovacs is the body of Elias Ryker, a disgraced former detective and partner/lover of Ortega.

An important sub-plot of the story is the fact that neo-Catholics are opposed to the idea of re-sleeving, holding that natural death is the only acceptable and moral outcome of life. They even oppose the practice of using the stack recovered after the death of the body to communicate with the person. This prevents the police from 'interviewing' victims of a crime in a virtual reality space, called 'spinning up'. Members of this religious group have their stacks digitally tagged to prevent this from happening.

The world of the twentieth-sixth century is also filled with artificial intelligence (AI), used in a variety of situations, as well as synthetic humans, cloning, and human enhancement.[31] Morgan weaves the plots of his three novels so that all of this is perfectly normal in context.

---

30. A note of caution if you have not yet read these books. The writing is graphic, both for the violence and sexual content.
31. Kovacs stays in a Bay City hotel, The Hendrix, that is entirely managed by AI. The persona of the hotel is the rock icon, Jimi Hendrix. Because of contractual issues, the hotel in the Netflix series is The Raven, and the AI persona is Poe.

So, What Does It Mean to be Human?

The three authors ask this question in different ways, and their answers are all quite distinct. The first two, Asimov and Dick, take the position that the 'other', whether robot or android/replicant, can be distinguished from human. The issues for them are if these creations can have something like consciousness and, more importantly, whether they are a threat to us or not. On the other hand, Morgan presents us with a real dilemma. How are we to think about the human in light of a world in which digitization and transfer of human consciousness is routinely practiced? I will deal with each of these issues in turn.

In his series of robot novels and short stories Asimov considers that these mechanical creations as distinct from us. The robots in the stories from which the movie, *I, Robot*, was taken are metallic creations that, while bipedal like us, look the part of an inorganic construct, made with a shiny skin and non-human face. In contrast, R Daneel Olivaw, the robot detective in *Caves of Steel* and the following novels is humanoid, visually indistinguishable from humans. In both cases, however, these artificial creatures are identifiably distinct from us in that they have no real internal experiences. Thus, they would fit Chalmers's philosophical zombie model. That is, when tested for objective correlates of consciousness, they would appear to pass the test. However, they would have no subjective experience.

This becomes the issue later on, especially with Sonny, the advanced robot in the movie *I, Robot*, who begins to be self-reflective and sees himself as both conscious and closer to human. Take this interchange between Detective Spooner and the robot, Sonny:

SPOONER: People generally believe that they have an immortal soul. If robots become intelligent, then the question of consciousness arises, and if a being is conscious, it becomes hard to deny it a soul -- and that sort of fouls up the whole thing for us. Do you understand?

THE ROBOT: People think God made them in His image.

SPOONER: That's the general belief.

THE ROBOT: And robots are made in the image of Man.

SPOONER: Right.

THE ROBOT: So that means robots are also the image of God. And I don't understand why God wouldn't want to give us immortal souls.

    (Spooner looks uncomfortable.)

SPOONER: Your reasoning has its points, but I'm afraid people will always see you as a collection of programming, a clockwork man. An illusion of life.

THE ROBOT: But that's not reasonable.

SPOONER: Isn't it? Can a robot take a blank canvas and paint a masterpiece? Can it write a poem that stirs the heart?

    (Long pause. Spooner waits. The Robot does not move. Then...)

THE ROBOT: Can *you* do either of those things?[32]

The androids/replicants of Dick's *Blade Runner* are a different case, but with the same outcome. Their consciousness is not disputed. But is it real or artificial? They were given implanted memories to simulate a lifetime, but they were only created a few years before. The task of the bounty hunter is to discern their true nature by looking at their empathic reactions. As an example of the Voight-Kampff test, look at this exchange between Deckard and Rachel, Eldon Tryell's niece who is an advanced model of a replicant:

(Rachael's eye fills the screen, the iris brilliant, shot with light, the pupil contracting. We hear Deckard's voice and we have the impression the test has been going on for a while.)

DECKARD: You are given a calfskin wallet for your birthday...
(Tyrell stands silhouetted behind Deckard, who sits in front of Rachael.)
(The needles in both gauges swing violently past green to red, then subside.)

RACHAEL: I wouldn't accept it, also I'd report the person who gave it to me to the police.

DECKARD: You have a little boy. He shows you his butterfly collection, plus the killing jar.

    (Again the gauges register, but not so far.)

---

32. *I, Robot* screenplay, located at https://www.simplyscripts.com/scripts/IrobotN. pdf, last accessed 3/19/19.

RACHAEL: I'd take him to the doctor.

DECKARD: You're watching TV and suddenly you notice a wasp crawling on your wrist.

RACHAEL: I'd kill it.

(Both needles go red. Deckard makes a note, takes a sip of coffee and continues.)

DECKARD: In a magazine you come across a full-page photo of a nude girl.

RACHAEL: Is this testing whether I'm a replicant or a lesbian?

DECKARD: You show the picture to your husband. He likes it and hangs it on the wall. The girl is lying on a bear-skin rug.

RACHAEL: I wouldn't let him.

DECKARD: Why not?

RACHAEL: I should be enough for him.

(Deckard frowns, then smiles. His smile looks a little like a grimace or the other way around.)

DECKARD: Last question. You're watching an old movie. It shows a banquet in progress, the guests are enjoying raw oysters.

RACHAEL: Ugh.

(Both needles swing swiftly.)

DECKARD: The entree consists of boiled dog stuffed with rice.

(Needles move less.)

DECKARD: *(continuing)* The raw oysters are less acceptable to you than a dish of boiled dog.

(Deckard switches off his beam.)[33]

This dialogue in the movie is very close to the same material in Dick's novel. It is taking a different tack than Asimov but comes to the same point relative to Chalmers's model. Replicants may be able to show some features of human subjective consciousness . . . for instance,

---

33. *Blade Runner* screenplay, located at http://www.dailyscript.com/scripts/blade-runner_shooting.html, last accessed 19/03/19.

memories . . . but they do not have internal reactions that dictate emotions such as empathy. Thus, they test again as philosophical zombies.

The truly challenging scenario is that portrayed in the Takeshi Kovacs novels of Morgan. Yes, there are robots, AI, synthetic beings and the like. However, we are presented with the world of DHF, the digitized, downloadable, and uploadable consciousness of each person that constitutes what we would normally consider the soul.

The Computation Theory of Mind (CTM) argues that what we perceive as cognition and consciousness is actually computation, in which the instrument that is used is the neural activity of the brain. The materialist view of the mind holds that brain states equal mental states. A more detailed statement would be that brain states are complex networks of neural synapses, the sum total of which constitutes the computational network that results in mental states.

There are at least six models of CTM, each of which fits philosophical features of consciousness more or less well.[34] In each of them, however, there is some appeal to the synaptic connections of the physical brain comprising the computation instrument of consciousness. In the world of Morgan's novels, it would be that complex network which can at long last be digitized and stored.

Of course, the Kovacs novels are fiction. However, there are companies currently in existence right now dedicated to achieving this same outcome. Carbon Copies is one such example.[35] Their Mission Statement includes the following:

> Ultimately, this means that we can reinvent our own mental processor, and that we can close the gap between human and machine. Our cognitive processes are then no longer tied to a single version of the brain's processing architecture. Instead, our thoughts and feelings will be able to exist on a variety of processing substrates. In that sense, we then have a substrate-independent mind (SIM). With advances in neuroscience and neural engineering we will be able to choose brain and body, much as we can choose winter or summer clothes to

---

34. Selvi Elif Gök and Erdinç Sayan, 'A philosophical assessment of computational models of consciousness', in *Cognitive Systems Research*, 17–18 (2012): 49–62.
35. Carbon Copies home page can be found at https://carboncopies.org, last accessed 19/03/19.

suit our needs. In science fiction, this possibility has been lightly explored in stories that involve 'mind uploading.' Neural prosthesis and whole brain emulation require accurate computational modeling of neural tissue, as well as developing neuromorphic hardware that is better suited to efficiently support the processes carried out in a neural architecture.[36]

Another example is Nectome,[37] whose home page states:

> Nectome is a research company dedicated to advancing the science of memory. We design and conduct experiments to discover how the brain physically creates memories. And, we develop biological preservation techniques to better preserve the physical traces of memory.[38]

Clearly, the long terms goals of these companies are a world much as described by Morgan with transhumanism propelled by leaps in technology. Therefore, the definition of what constitutes the human person comes immediately to the front of the discussion.

Indeed, the idea of digitising human consciousness has been the subject of recent speculation and discussion. *Intelligence Unbound: The Future of Uploaded and Machine Minds* is an anthology of contributions by scientists, futurists, ethicists, and philosophers.[39] Two of the articles in this anthology strike at the heart of my discussion. The first is by David Chalmers, whom we've already reviewed with respect to the 'hard problem' of the mind-body question. The second, by Massimo Pigliucci, is a critical response to Chalmers.

David Chalmers takes on the philosophical issues of mind uploading in his contribution.[40] He divides the discussion into two questions:

1) If my consciousness is uploaded to a computer, will it still be conscious?
2) If my consciousness is uploaded, will it still be me?

---

36. Carbon Copies home page can be found at https://carboncopies.org, last accessed 19/03/19.
37. Nectome home page is found at https://nectome.com, last accessed 19/03/19.
38. Nectome home page is found at https://nectome.com, last accessed 19/03/19.
39. Russell Blackford and Damien Broderick, *Intelligence Unbound: The Future of Uploaded and Machine Minds* (Oxford: Wiley Blackwell, 2014).
40. David Chalmers, 'Uploading: A Philosophical Analysis', in Blackford and Broderick, *Intelligence Unbound: The Future of Uploaded and Machine Minds* (Oxford: Wiley Blackwell, 2014), 101–118.

The answer to these questions depends upon whether or not one thinks of consciousness in a biological or functional sense. Biological theorists contend that consciousness requires a biological structure and therefore that a non-biological system cannot exhibit this property. Functional theorists, on the other hand, argue that consciousness requires a causal structure and a causal role. Therefore, a correctly structured non-biological system can have this property.

Chalmers maintains that 'functionalist theories are closer to the truth'. Recall that he maintains that mind cannot be explained completely by brain states (his philosophical zombie test). However, he seems to maintain in this paper that whatever the qualia issues of our internal experience of consciousness might be, this would transfer intact during mind uploading.

I'm actually perplexed by this. Chalmers claims that our subjected internal experience cannot be reduced to the physical brain state. And yet, by digitising that brain state . . . that is, by creating a precise digital record of all synaptic connections and any other relevant cellular interactions . . . an upload of our consciousness and even personal continuity to a computer would be possible. How is the digital record different from the brain states of which they are a kind of map? What makes it a sort of qualia and not a quantified computation?

Massimo Pigliucci deals with some of these arguments in his contribution to the anthology.[41] However, as a biological theorist, he then falls into the trap of assuming that brain states will be determinative of mental states. He does not state this directly, but rather argues that for consciousness to exist, there must be biological components of the brain that cannot be duplicated by circuitry in a computer. That is, consciousness is substrate-dependent.

My critique of these two approaches is that both of these philosophers of mind are riding roughshod over the subject of the nature of mind behind three of those four horsemen we encountered earlier: materialism, physicalism, and scientism. While they may have abandoned one of the riders, reductionism, in favor of the more popular systems approach to understanding biological systems, they are still firmly in stride with the other three. It is from this position that they

---

41. Massimo Pigliucci, 'Mind Uploading: A Philosophical Counter-Analysis', in Blackford and Broderick, *Intelligence Unbound: The Future of Uploaded and Machine Minds* (Oxford: Wiley Blackwell, 2014), 118–130.

try to conclude that digital versions of brain states might, in any way, be equivalent to consciousness and, in fact, personality.

The transhumanist movement that sees mind uploading as the ultimate pathway to immortality is also imbedded in this philosophical milieu. Of course, proponents ignore the idea put forth by Aristotle and later commented on by St Thomas Aquinas that humans are rational animals with a soul, defined as the formal cause of what it means to be human. Of course, the materialists belittle this view as 'neo-scholastic'.[42] To deny the existence of the non-material is, in fact, circular reasoning at its worst. Science can only observe the material world. Science has never observed the non-material soul. Therefore, the non-material soul does not exist. Take that, neo-scholastics!

The transhumanist paradise, perhaps as depicted in the world of *Altered Carbon*, would, to my non-uploaded mind, be populated by sophisticated versions of Chalmersian zombies. Thanks, but no thanks.

---

42. Pigliucci, 'Mind Uploading: A Philosophical Counter-Analysis', 129, footnote 4.

On the Faith of Droids

Daniel J Peterson

'I think he's searching for his former master, but I've never seen such devotion in a droid before.'
– Luke Skywalker, *Star Wars: A New Hope*

Abstract. Theologians and biblical scholars have attempted in different ways to define what constitutes within or among human beings the image of God, the *imago Dei*. These efforts, as Noreen Herzfeld argues, can be useful in looking at how designers of AI have attempted to fashion AI in their image. Absent the discussion, however, is the consideration of how faith, which according to Paul Tillich makes personality possible, might be reflected in AI. Faith is the condition for the possibility of Strong AI. Since Strong AI does not yet exist, the present essay analyzes its appearance in the genre of science fiction film, specifically in the characters of R2-D2 (*Star Wars: A New Hope*) and K2-SO (*Rogue One: A Star Wars Story*), showing how faith as a trait/capacity and as an expression of relationship both contribute to the *imago hominis* in Strong AI and help make Strong AI possible.

Key Terms. Artificial Intelligence (AI), *Imago Dei*, Paul Tillich, *Rogue One, Star Wars*

Bio. Daniel J Peterson is pastor of Queen Anne Lutheran Church in Seattle. Formerly a member of the faculty at Pacific Lutheran University and Seattle University, he is the author of *Tillich: A Brief Introduction to the Life and Writings of Paul Tillich* (Minneapolis: Lutheran University Press, 2013) and co-editor of *Resurrecting the Death of God: The Origins, Influence and Return of Radical Theology* (Albany: SUNY Press, 2014).

Genesis 1:1–2:4a, the first account of creation in the Hebrew Bible, offers much to ponder: a world that that blooms with vegetation in the blink of a day (vv11–12); the appearance of light *before* God hangs the stars onto the ceiling of the nighttime sky (vv 3, 14–18); seas that teem almost instantaneously with life (v 20); a sublime depiction of God in refreshingly non-anthropomorphic terms as a mighty wind that sweeps across waters of primeval chaos, dark and deep (v 2). Yet at the heart of this, the Priestly version of the world at its inception, lies two verses that have garnered more attention than any of the above combined, namely, the claim that God made human beings in God's image (Gen 1:26–27).

Genesis 1:26–27 lends itself to multiple interpretive possibilities. It speaks of God in the plural, suggesting to some commentators that the image of God or *imago Dei* resides not so much within us as the freedom of the will or the capacity to reason, but among us when we live in harmony with one another. Others, including the biblical scholar Gerhard von Rad, think of the *imago Dei* as the unique role human beings have in exercising dominion over creation and caring for it on God's behalf (Gen 1:28).[1] Still others, having defined what it means to bear the divine image, question whether any of it even remains after Adam's fall in the second biblical account of creation (Gen 3:22–24). The sixteenth century theologian John Calvin, for example, emphasizes the severity of the fall to such an extent that nothing of God's image survives Adam's transgression and expulsion from paradise, rendering the search for a meaningful definition ultimately moot. Fortunately, at least for the sake of discussion, Noreen Herzfeld assumes otherwise.

For Herzfeld, author of *In Our Image: Artificial Intelligence and the Human Spirit*, exploring the ways in which Hebrew Bible scholars and Christian theologians interpret the meaning of the *imago Dei* has a dual significance. It not only sheds light on how we understand ourselves, especially when it comes to what we cherish most about being human. It also illuminates what we hope to replicate of ourselves in the creation of strong artificial intelligence (AI), that is, as Ted Peters explains elsewhere in the present volume, 'a machine capable of performing any task the human brain can perform'. The goal that informs such research, Herzfeld argues, springs from the desire to create something that mirrors us, 'to build something *like* ourselves'.

---

1. Noreen Herzfeld, *In Our Image: Artificial Intelligence and the Human Spirit* (Minneapolis: Fortress Press, 2002), 21–24.

Thus, 'as the *imago Dei* captures the way humans are like God, so the *imago hominis* of artificial intelligence seeks to capture the way computers could be like humans'.[2] Herzfeld's analysis shows, in turn, how researchers in the field of AI have sought to endow machines with the ennobling qualities, capacities, and functions biblical exegetes and theologians attribute to the divine image within (or among) us as human beings.

Nothing thus far sounds problematic until we recall, as John Calvin points out, that the second account of creation, the Yahwist account in Genesis 2–4, ends in a breach between God and human beings, one God presumably does not intend. If that happens when God creates human beings in God's image, imagine what disasters might result when human beings create AI in their image! Strong AI would not, as in Genesis, fall away from the perfection of a wholly benevolent deity; it would, rather, duplicate the morally ambiguous, even sinful nature of its all-too-human progenitors. As Alan Weissenbacher remarks elsewhere in the present volume, 'Humans will pass their penchant for sin onto their creations, and to think that a sufficient super-intelligence will see these sins and avoid them, or care about avoiding them, is the height of wishful thinking'. Any technological creation capable of imitating our best qualities will, in short, also have the potential to embody our worst.

These qualities vary considerably. The substantive approach, which Herzfeld identifies as the dominant way theologians historically have interpreted the image of God, equates it with a special capacity or trait of human nature, including everything from self-transcendence and reason to free will and our personality.[3] The introduction of sin complicates matters. It corrupts and distorts the aforementioned qualities, producing an additional capacity, say, for selfishness or pride, disclosing in the process a sharp contrast between what it means to exist in the *imago hominis* versus the *imago Dei*. Being made in the *imago Dei*, at least, allows for the theoretical possibility of a life without sin, which biblical and creedal Christianity affirms concerning Christ, whereas being made in the *imago hominis* makes sin, to use the language of Reinhold Niebuhr, not only inevitable but necessary. Robots, it would seem, have no hope.

2. Herzfeld, *In Our Image*, 50.
3. Herzfeld, *In Our Image*, 16.

Fortunately, for robots on the big screen, theological consistencies need not apply. AI in cinema can be unambiguously good, as in the case of the character WALL-E in the 2008 film of the same name, even if its maker is flawed. It can alternatively be evil, deceptive and destructive without explanation, as in the case of HAL from *2001: A Space Odyssey* or more recently the character of Ava in Alex Garland's *Ex Machina*. AI on screen, moreover, occasionally demonstrates another possibility for its future, possessing, as in the character of R2-D2 in *Star Wars*, a sense of mission or what appears to be the rudiments of *faith*, a faculty or capacity of special interest to theologians, yet one Herzfeld curiously neglects in her treatment of the topic.[4] Could AI ever develop the capacity to exhibit what the German American theologian Paul Tillich calls an ultimate concern? Could a droid have a relationship with God?

Faith Forming Self

Absent the emergence presently of Strong AI, why pursue the topic any further if the analysis must by necessity restrict itself to science fiction? Two reasons come to mind. First, fiction has the potential to shape the future, revealing new possibilities for exploration to researchers. The once-popular flip phone, novel for its time, had its antecedent in the make-believe communicators the crew of the Enterprise used in the original *Star Trek* television series. Second, exploring the potential pitfalls and perks of computer super-intelligence as it confronts us in film may help us more effectively prepare for its actual appearance, should it one day arrive. What happens, for example, if by fluke or by design a robot manifested a sense of allegiance or devotion to a person, group, or cause? How might we react?

Paul Tillich witnessed the horrific effects of faith understood as unquestioning devotion to a particular group while living in Germany in the 1920s and early 1930s. Faith, he came to realize, is not about believing in certain religious doctrines. It involves, rather, being

---

4. This could be, as I elaborate further below, because faith belongs neither entirely to the various faculties interpreters link with the divine image in human beings, including our capacity for reason or self-transcendence, nor wholly to the relational model of the *imago Dei*, particularly as Karl Barth presents. Instead, to use a well-worn phrase from Paul Tillich, it resides on the boundary between the two.

'grasped' by something that brings with it a demand and promise, both of which the subject experiences as unconditional. Theoretically, all people have faith insofar as they do more than simply live—they live *for* something, and that 'something' functionally serves as their god. The question, then, is not whether people believe in god, but in which god they place their trust and allegiance. What do they value above all else? What matters most in their lives? Is it money, social status, climbing the corporate ladder, romantic love, the nation, or God? Obviously, in some cases the object that becomes an ultimate concern (for example, money) is not intrinsically evil, but when it takes on the status of being unconditionally important or the reason for one's being, it can be highly destructive to others as well as oneself (*cf* 1 Tim 6:6–10). 'The risk to faith in one's ultimate concern is indeed the greatest risk man can run', Tillich writes. 'For if it proves to be a failure, the meaning of one's life breaks down; one surrenders oneself . . . to something which is not worth it.'[5]

Beyond the important claim that faith orients the individual toward something he or she takes with unconditional significance as opposed merely to believing that something is true, Tillich offers another observation particularly relevant to our purposes. Faith, he says, integrates mind, heart, and will in a centered act of the personality, effectively making personality possible by directing it toward the singular object of its concern (20). Lloyd Geering in *Reimagining God* claims likewise, albeit with regard to the broader development of Western consciousness historically thanks to monotheism. 'The theologian Gordon Kaufman', he remarks, 'pointed out that the concept of God, apart from the now outmoded images, has long served as a unifying point to which we can orient everything else and so make sense of the world and our place in it' (128). Even if God has 'died' in modern secular society, Geering concludes, the idea proved useful. It gave us focus. Around it and because of it we constructed our world, emerging individually and collectively from the 'jumble of sense impressions . . . to become more mature, integrated selves, a process [Carl] Jung termed individuation.'[6]

---

5. Paul Tillich, *The Dynamics of Faith* (New York: Harper & Row, 1957), 17.
6. Lloyd Geering, *Reimaging God: The Faith Journey of a Modern Heretic* (Salem: Polebridge Press, 2017), 137.

The significance of Tillich's position in relation to the development of Strong AI should thus be clear. Faith creates the self in human beings. It makes personality possible by integrating and uniting its various functions in the service of a single-minded focus. If robots were bound as well by a sense of mission or what matters most, either as a result of their programming or because of what the biologist Stephen Jay Gould calls a 'fortunate fluke' in reference to *our* evolutionary past, could such a focus, itself perhaps a rudimentary expression of ultimate concern, contribute to an emerging sense of interiority, to the robot's growing sense of self? Might such a robot, the kind driven by a fledgling ultimate concern, eventually pass the Turing Test? Could it, beyond its relationship with human beings, develop a capacity to relate to the maker of its maker, to God? Could faith be the key that unlocks the doorway to Strong AI?

Two Candidates for Consideration: R2-D2 and K2-SO

We only have one significant clue. At the beginning of *Star Wars: A New Hope*, shortly after her ship has been besieged, Princess Leia inserts a small disc into R2-D2, one of the two main 'droids' in the film. The disc contains the stolen plans of the Empire's new leathal weapon, the Death Star. The scene takes place without words.

Sometime later, R2D2's new owner, Luke Skywalker, discovers the plans irretrievably wedged inside the droid, accidentally playing a message the droid refuses to repeat. Thus begins a litany of explanations on the part of R2's counterpart, C3-PO, who attributes the former droid's bizarre behavior to the hardships both of them have endured together over time, only later to claim that the fault lies presumably in R2's programming. 'These astrodroids are getting quite out of hand', he says to Luke after R2 escapes to fulfill his mission. 'Even I can't understand their logic sometimes.' The variety of explanations keeps the viewer guessing: does R2's sense of mission to get the plans to another character (Obi-Wan Kenobi), one that inspires Luke to say he's 'never seen such devotion in a droid before', stem from a malfunction, as C3-PO's comments seem to suggest, or was it programmed by Princess Leia?

Regardless of its source, a spark exists, a faculty, whether by accident or by intention, that provides the condition for the possibility of

R2's faith or what Herzfeld nicely calls his 'dogged loyalty'.[7] Yet how do we explain that fact that once R2's mission is complete, once he delivers the recording and the plans, such loyalty expands in relation to other characters, especially Luke? Could it be that it grows out of the relationships of interdependence he and Luke develop, illustrating how faith exists on the boundary between the substantive approach to the *imago Dei*, which again identifies the image of God in human beings with a particular faculty, and what Herzfeld subsequently presents as the relational approach to the *imago Dei*, which indicates that we mirror the triune God when we find ourselves in mutual relationship with God and/or one another?[8]

A more developed expression of ultimate concern appears in K2-SO, a former imperial security droid who appears in 2016's *Rogue One: A Star Wars Story*. Critics give him more accolades than any other character of the film, in several cases with obvious irony. Richard Brody, who scorches everything in the movie from the direction of the actors to the 'flat and inexpressive' script, nevertheless finds kind words for the droid. 'The one character with any inner-identity is, in fact, a robot', he says, 'K2-SO, voiced by Alan Tudyk, and the only performance with any flair at all is a CGI incarnation, or rather, resurrection'.[9] Notice here the reference to 'inner-identity', a hallmark of Strong AI. Another critic, Eric Goldman, refers likewise to the 'sympathetic soul' Tudyk's performance gives to K2, adding playfully, 'if such a word [soul] is appropriate for a droid' (fn). What do we make of that? How did K2 get a 'sympathetic soul' in the first place?

K2 has an intriguing back-story. Cassian Andor, a pilot and member of the Rebel Alliance, reprogrammed him. Before that, K2 was an imperial security droid who emerges as the major source of comic relief throughout the film. Upon meeting Jyn Erso, the film's protagonist, K2 comments, rather dryly, 'The captain says you are a friend. I will not kill you'. Cassian, meanwhile, seems at a loss when it comes to explaining his creation's humor. "He tends to say whatever he wants', he shares with Jyn, 'whatever is in his circuits. It's a by-product of

7. Herzfeld, *In Our Image*, 62.
8. Herzfeld, *In Our Image*, 31.
9. Richard Brody, '"Rogue One" Reviewed: Is it Time to Abandon the Star Wars Francise?', in *The New Yorker*, accessed 2/10/19. https://www.newyorker.com/culture/richard-brody/rogue-one-reviewed-is-it-time-to-abandon-the-star-wars-franchise

his reprogramming'. Critics likewise offer their best guesses regarding the source of his humor. 'K2-50 [sic] was also apparently given a sarcasm chip, and a complete set of *The Hitchhiker's Guide to the Galaxy*', jokes Chris Barsanti, 'all the better to model his behavior on that of Marvin the Paranoid Android'.[10] Like R2, K2 appears at first to have some kind of faculty that helps explains his humanlike eccentricities—a capacity, whether intentional or a by-product—concerning the *imago hominis* within him.

Yet as the film progresses, K2's loyalty to Cassian, including the cause which Cassian serves, grows significantly, so much so that it culminates in the droid's self-sacrifice, the first of its kind we see in any film of the *Star Wars* franchise. Tudyk, the actor who plays the character, offers a persuasive explanation accordingly. 'For all his rough edges, Kaytoo also feels fierce loyalty', he says, 'especially toward . . . Cassian . . . who cleared the droids databanks of Imperial programming and and allowed him to break free of service to the galactic dictatorship.' The source of K2's loyalty suddenly becomes clear. "He wants what Cassian wants," Tudyk continues. 'He loves Cassian because Cassian freed him. It's also more paternal in that [Cassian] gave him life and took away the bonds of his programming.'[11] The theological overtones could not be more apparent: K2, out of gratitude for the gift of life and freedom, makes Cassian and by extension the rebel cause his ultimate concern. Relationship once again provides the context out of which the created reflects the image of its creator, the result of which gives our droid his reason for being. Cassian and his cause become the god(s) whom K2 serves.

In Ephesians the same logic of faith appears, only this time obviously with respect to human beings and their ideal relationship with God. 'All of us', the author declares, 'once lived among [the disobedient] in the passions of our flesh, following the desires of flesh and senses, and we were by nature children of wrath, like everyone else' (2:3). We were bound, 'slaves of sin', as Paul says in Romans 6:17. But now, thanks to the gift of God's grace (Eph 2:8), we are liberated, 'made . . . alive together with Christ', the appropriate response

---

10. Chris Barsanti, "*Rogue One: A Star Wars Story* Shows There's Life in *Star Wars* Yet…Barely," *PopMatters*, accessed 2/10/19. https://www.popmatters.com/rogue-one-star-wars-story-theres-life-in-star-wars-yet-barely-2495405800.html

11. Anthony Breznican, *Entertainment Weekly*, accessed 2/10/19. https://ew.com/article/2016/08/10/rogue-one-alan-tudyk/

to which is thanksgiving (5:4, 20), good works (2:10), and single-minded devotion to God (that is, faith) whom we can approach in boldness and with confidence through Jesus Christ our Lord (3:11).

Implications for Understanding AI and Ourselves

R2 and K2 offer snapshots of what Strong AI could like should it ever appear. Both droids exhibit varying degrees of faith, of single-minded devotion that becomes increasingly evident in their actions and arguably makes possible or at least deepens their respective personalities. At first, other characters offer explanations concerning the source of their quirky, human-like behavior (R2's stubborn persistence, K2's sarcasm). These, however, merely scratch the surface, ultimately burning off as both films pass like starships through the atmosphere. By the time they reach the ground, particularly *Rogue One*, we see how the more profoundly human qualities of love and self-sacrifice emerge out of relationship rather than rewiring. K2 imbibes the best of humanity by doing for Cassion and Jyn what Christ did for all people, giving himself up so that others might live.

The comparison, of course, is not perfect! K2 employs violence in the service of his faith, that is, his unwavering commitment to Cassian and the cause, yet it seems that by the end of the film it is his faith that enables him to determine concretely and powerfully who he is and what he must do. Is it such faith, understood as a centering act of single-minded focus, that lures K2's inchoate personality out of his sub-concious circuitry? If so, does the possibility exist that he, now free, has the option to turn away from Cassian and the cause in rebellion, just as Adam turns away from God at the edge of the Garden? Could this, taking seriously now the penchant for sin human beings would automatically pass on to their creations, be their downfall? How might this reflect our humanity back to us? Do we like what we see, and if we do not, what steps, if any, can we take to prevent occurring in robots what we find maddeningly occurring within ourselves?

Our focus on R2 and K2, finally, raises another question. What about the rest of the droids that populate the *Star Wars* universe, if not the various other droids of science fiction generally, including Replicants in the *Blade Runner* films? By leaving them out of our present discussion and focusing exclusively on what Herzfeld calls the 'genre of companionable artificial intelligence', what might we be avoiding or repressing about who we are that we must confront?[12] Genesis 1, the Priestly account of creation, implies only possibilities for the good when it comes to affirming that God makes human beings in God's image. We must also consider Genesis 2–3, the Yahwist account of creation, for a more sobering look at who we are but also what we, fancying ourselves to be God rather than human beings who bear the image of God, could create. K2, after all, began not as Cassian's co-pilot but as a security droid—a security droid for the empire.

Conclusion

Intelligence without centering by faith is nothing more than calculation. In fact, it's not intelligence at all.

R2 and K2 illustrate fully embodied robotic intelligence. They provide a working image of what Strong AI would be like should it ever appear. Here is what is significant: these droids exhibit varying degrees of faith, of single-minded devotion that becomes increasingly evident in their actions and arguably makes possible or at least deepens their respective personalities.

Regardless of what theologians surmise about the *imago Dei* attached to *Homo sapiens,* we can see that it is faith which orients the self and constructs personhood. Intelligence is a function of personhood in the human being. If Strong AI is ever to attain intelligence in emulation of the human, then a faith-centered personhood will be requisite.

---

12. Herzfeld, *In Our Image*, 63.

From Heidegger on Technology to an Inclusive Puralistic Theology

Rajesh Sampath

The 'essence of technology is not itself technological.'
– Martin Heidegger[1]

Abstract. This article explores Heidegger's later philosophy and what this means for possible theological interpretations of the relationship between humans and automated technology, especially Artificial Intelligence (AI). The essay concludes with prospects for *an inclusive pluralistic theology*, which may require the de-centering of the 'natural, biological human' as the highest manifestation of God's creation.

Keywords. Heidegger, AI, technology, theological ethics, philosophy of religion

Bio. Rajesh Sampath is Associate Professor of the Philosophy of Justice, Rights, and Social Change at Brandeis University.

This article explores Heidegger's later philosophy and what that means for possible theological interpretations of the relationship between humans and automated technology, such as Artificial Intelligence (AI). We will inquire into the possibility, limits, and hope for faith in a futuristic age.

The paper has three parts. First, I will explore ethical arguments for or against the possibility of AI superseding human intelligence and making moral decisions on its own. This will set up the question: Could AI have non-natural rights to faith? Would this right obtain when faith's boundaries with reason become blurred? Will the limits

---

1. Martin Heidegger, 'Question Concerning Technology', in *Basic Writings*, edited by David Farrell Krell (New York: Harper Perennial, 2008), 311.

of theological norms become strained when non-human fidelity to traditional doctrines of the Christian God are tested?

In the second part, I will utilise Heidegger's philosophical investigations of technology as a prism to explore the theological question: what does AI/machine technology imply for Christian anthropology?

In the third part of the paper I will offer a thought experiment. How might an AI program have its own interpretation of the New Testament message? How might an intelligent machine read the Gospels? How might Heidegger's framing of the issues help us navigate the moral perplexity of a non-human relationship to God?

This essay concludes with prospects for *an inclusive pluralistic theology*, one that includes rather than excludes intelligent machines within our spiritual community. Such an inclusive pluralistic theology may require the de-centering of the natural, biological human; it may require an unseating of humanity from its inherited throne as the highest manifestation of God's creation.

Debates about AI

This first part will briefly summarise arguments for or against AI. Is artificial intelligence really intelligent? Humanlike? Supra-human?

One can ask whether non-natural or human-constructed, mechanical technologies can and will surpass natural, biological human intelligence. But that could be an ethically neutral scientific question that only scientists and technologists can debate given the technical, mathematical, computation and neuroscientific complexity of the subject.[2]

A step further would be whether a non-human machine intelligence could develop a religious and moral capacity, to feel guilt and sin along with salvation and redemption. This question is more pertinent for our investigation, albeit speculative. No one today would grant that AI is already at the level of basic human cognition with or without capacity for religious feeling or the pursuit of meaning and ultimate truth. So, let us go with the hypothetical scenario. A subset question would be this: would it be morally good or bad if AI were to develop a religious sensibility for transcendence? A soul?

---

2. Stuart Russell and Peter Norvig, *Artificial Intelligence: A Modern Approach*, 3rd Edition (Essex: Pearson Education Limited, 2014).

Here is a problem for the theologian: our religious traditions have presumed that the human soul makes the human more than an animal. The soul defines the human species as the crown of creation. The human is the preeminent of all of God's creatures endowed with sovereignty over others: all animals and plants (Gen 1:26). Furthermore, God breathed into his paramount creation from the dust, and the human became a 'living soul' (Gen 2:7). Reformer John Calvin speaks for the dominant Christian tradition: 'When [God's] image is placed in man a tacit antithesis is introduced which raises man above all other creatures and, as it were, separates him from the common mass.'[3] Now let us ask: Would a religious and moral robot with a soul become a rival to the human throne?

If our biblically inherited hierarchy is thrown off by the invention of AI superior to *Homo sapiens*, then traditional faith would start to unravel. If an AI robot would rise to a level of intelligence or morality or religiosity higher than the human, might it rise into the very domain of the divine? Might AI climb the technological Tower of Babel to invade the heavens? Shall we, as Yuval Harari advocates, 'now aim to upgrade humans into gods, and turn *Homo sapiens* into *Homo deus*'?[4]

This would be theologically problematic, to say the least. Christians have long assumed that no reasoning human'—except God incarnate in Jesus Christ, the preexistent Logos from the standpoint of Christian faith (Jn 1:1–18)—could ever attain the very omniscience or omnipotence of God. What must be maintained, traditionally, is the protection of a sacred distinction central to faith, namely God's unsurpassable transcendence as a mystery.[5]

So what do these standard theological ruminations entail about the fact that technology has *already* arrived and that there is a good chance a superior technology may be born in the future, one that

---

3. John Calvin, *Institutes of the Christian Religion* (1559), edited by John T. McNeill, *Library of Christian Classics* XX, XXI (Louisville: Westminster John Knox Press, 1960) I, xv, 3, 188.

4. Yuval Noah Harari, *Homo Deus: A Brief History of Tomorrow* (New York: Harper, 2017), 21.

5. In recent Christian anthropology, the key human trait is openness to transcendence. When God becomes revealed, what is revealed is that God is mystery. Knowledge of God is knowledge of this transcendent mystery. This is characteristic of Karl Rahner, Karl Barth, and Wolfhart Pannenberg.

could replace the human as the center or apex of all creation? It could mean that the very act of creating AI could lead to this usurpation of God's power, which could then deform traditional doctrines of faith to the point of an indiscernible heresy. Both God's eschatological omnipotence (and human's special responsibility to non-humans until that crescendo point of historical time arrives) would dissolve. Therein lies the most profound dilemma that many religious people may have to confront.

We will explore this *aporia*. In order to do so, we must acknowledge that some among us see AI's ultimate supersession of human reason as a superior mode of reasoning on earth as inevitable and good.[6] Others see the danger in this, which can distort human to human relationships and potentially threaten the existence of all biological life in the future. Therefore, we must proceed with 'caution' even though we cannot instantaneously leap out of this technological age.[7] Indeed, there is no point in asking whether we should try to take this leap seeing that it may not be possible even if we so desired. In this paper I argue that before we take a stand on the necessity for precautionary sobriety at minimum or maintenance of human preeminence at maximum (with regard to dominion over all non-humans, animals, plants, technological automatons, biotechnological hybrids, etc), let us turn to the insights of the twentieth century continental European philosopher, Martin Heidegger (1889–1976). We will see how he tries to frame the question of technology in terms of authentic humanity, outside the context of mainstream theology and Anglo-American analytic social ethics discussions.

On Heidegger's 'Question Concerning Technology'

In this second part we will offer a brief critical analysis and interpretation of Heidegger's influential essay, 'Questioning Concerning Technology' (1957). This important text has shaped many moral,

---

6. Timothy Revell, 'AI will be able to beat us at everything by 206, says experts', in *New Scientist* (May 31st, 2017); https://www.newscientist.com/article/2133188-ai-will-be-able-to-beat-us-at-everything-by-2060-say-experts/.

7. See Noreen Herzfeld's 'The Enchantment of Artificial Intelligence' and Ted Peter's 'Artificial Intelligence, Transhumanism, and Frankenfear'. Both articles appear in this volume.

ethical, and philosophical debates about the virtues and dangers of technological progress.[8]

My analysis in this section reaffirms traditional scholarly assumptions. For one, Heidegger is not advocating for some nostalgic or romantic return to a pre-Newtonian/classical mechanical and therefore pre-industrial age when today's automated technologies were not possible.[9] But nor does this impossibility to time travel back to a more 'innocent' age lead—necessarily—to a nihilistic or atheistic future where religion and theology become permanently obsolete. Rather, I will argue for a space of the holy and divine to be possible but only after reading Heidegger's take on the age of technology. For this German philosopher is asking us to consider the following: once we admit to the potential dangers of a non-thinking relationship to the *essence* of technology, an essence which is never technological in itself,[10] and we humans have no foreseeable way to stop the onslaught of technological command over everything, we still have a special ethical responsibility.

Indeed, Heidegger asks us to reorient our very Being/essence to technology in ways that can handle the deepest mysteries of the human condition—that is, towards an appropriate type of thinking-orienting receptiveness about what can 'save' us so that we don't completely annihilate the possibility for a redemptive event to occur. What is that redemptive event? It is the event in which 'truth comes to pass.'[11]

Heidegger is seeking what he calls a 'free' relationship that 'opens our human existence to the essence of technology.'[12] But as mentioned previously, the 'essence of technology is not itself technological.'[13]

---

8. See Robert C. Sharff and Val Dusek, editors, *The Philosophy of Technology: The Technological Condition- An Anthology* (Oxford: Wiley Blackwell, 2014), 503–647.
9. See the works of Andrew Feenberg (1991, 1995, 1999, 2002, 2005, 2010, 2017), Iain Thomson (2005), and Don Idhe (1979, 1983, 1998, and 2010).
10. Heidegger, 'Question Concerning Technology', 311.
11. Heidegger, 'Question Concerning Technology', 333. In reference to a phrase in a Hölderlin poem, Heidegger refers to this the 'saving power.' How we think about that can help prepare how we can even receive a response to the dangers of not thinking essentially about the very essence of technology and what that means for the fate of human beings.
12. Heidegger, 'Question Concerning Technology', 311.
13. Heidegger, 'Question Concerning Technology', 311.

That means we can't really turn to how natural scientists or technology entrepreneurs (Google, Facebook, Apple, Microsoft, IBM) define technology. Furthermore, this would also include social scientists who use positivistic and empirical epistemological frameworks to understand human beings' relationship to technology, for example the utility and policy dimensions of stem cell research to manufacture organs. Rather, Heidegger is thinking in the broadest philosophical terms, which stretches back to his earliest reflections up to his masterpiece, *Being and Time* (1927).[14]

Beyond the natural and social sciences, we also can't turn to the history of Western metaphysical attempts to define 'human beings', let alone 'their essence' or what the Being of the beings that are humans even means.[15] Finally, traditional theological doctrines of Christianity are inadmissible for the Heidegger of *Being and Time*.[16] But this is not an investigation of Heidegger's philosophical critique of religion or the possibilities for a Heideggerean philosophy of religion.

All I want to do here is draw some preliminary observations. Since we cannot start with any assumption of what the human being even means, we can't just dive into debates about whether human beings should (say in a normative ethical sense) embrace technology. Some examples include gene editing of fetuses or cloning, which bioethi-

---

14. Martin Heidegger, *Being and Time*, translated by John Macquerrie and Edward Robinson (New Yorker, Harper and Row, 1963).

15. For example, the incredibly complex notion of the *Imago Dei* or man made in God's image in Genesis 1:26. 'Created in the image of God, human beings are by nature bodily and spiritual, men and women made for one another, persons oriented towards communion with God and with one another, wounded by sin and in need of salvation, and destined to be conformed to Christ, the perfect image of the Father, in the power of the Holy Spirit.' Vatican: International Theological Commission, *Communion and Stewardship: Human Persons Created in the Image of God 2002*, http://www.vatican.ca/roman_curia/congregations/cfaith/cti_documents/rc_con_cfaith_doc.

16. Before 1927, Heidegger had given up on dogmatic faith and institutional commitments to being Catholic. This does not mean he did not have a life-long, complex relationship with religion and theology before and after his break, for example his dialogues with the Lutheran theologian Rudolf Bultmann in the early 20s during his time in Marburg. See Benjamin Crowe, *Heidegger's Religious Origins: Destruction and Authenticity* (Bloomington: Indiana University Press, 2006).

cists have to debate.[17] Nor are we considering that humans should fatalistically abandon themselves to technological supremacy, knowing full-well that they can't escape its near ubiquitous presence on earth.[18] In the latter sense, we may have to accept the idea that we may be one of many creatures on earth in the future, particularly if an alien encounter ever happens. But even in the chance of that stupendous world-historical event doesn't mean we humans will be required to abandon faith and theology.[19] But these are not the questions before us.

It seems what is really at stake for Heidegger is the idea of a 'free relation' and 'openness' to the 'essence of technology', which is never technological. (Encountering aliens for example assumes we or they would have to have some advance technology to travel through real Einsteinian space-time, which would then require a reckoning of the nature of that technology. As of now we humans have never traveled through a wormhole and back.[20]) Yet, Heidegger is not interested in actual technologies or imagined ones in science fiction. Furthermore, his questioning is also irreducible to the history of metaphysics and theology; the latter fields have the capacity to think about essence in its highest generality, say the relationship between human and God, or human and transcendence, which goes beyond all sensorial and empirical reality. Long story short, after Heidegger winds his way from the ancient Greeks' idea of *techne* to his modern context, he lands on a definition of this 'essence' of technology as *Gestell*, which is translated as "Enframing" from his original German.[21]

Whether we like technology or not is not the issue. Whether we think humans create technology is not the issue either; for that goes

17. Helga Kuhse, Udo Schüklenk, and Peter Singer, editors *Bioethics*, 3rd Edition (Oxford: Wiley Blackwell, 2016), 173.
18. Heidegger, 'Question Concerning Technology', 311. There Heidegger says affirming or denying technology is useless.
19. Ted Peters, Martinez Hewlett, Joshua M Moritz, and Robert John Russell, editors., *Astrotheology: Science and Theology Meet Extraterrestrial Life* (Eugene: Cascade Books, 2018). Theological reflections of this kind hold enormous importance for the future of the religion and science dialogue and its commensurability with faith.
20. This is still the realm of science fiction like Christopher Nolan's magnificent film, *Interstellar* (2014) on which Nobel Prize winning Caltech physicist, Kip Thorne, consulted.
21. Heidegger, 'Questioning Concerning Technology', 324.

without saying as a simple fact since the dawn of the Industrial Age. Rather, Heidegger is concerned with that 'free relation' that 'opens human existence' to an essence. Since *Being and Time*, Heidegger has had the ambition to go beyond the history of Western thought, and so no existing sense of what that 'essence' entails is available in anything other than what Heidegger is trying to articulate, and often times in his own inventive neologisms. Since in the modern age, unlike previous epochs, technology seems to dominate the mode by which we exist (say unlike a pastoral or agrarian antiquity), then the essence of technology is not obscured by these basic claims: a.) technology is complex and scary and can spin out of control; b.) technology is the panacea for all human suffering; c.) we have yet to arrive at a true understanding of technology that has to go beyond the history of all human conceptions even though it will be our salvation. Rather, for Heidegger, the real challenge that is engulfing human beings is a 'claim that gathers man with a view to ordering the self-revealing as standing-reserve: *Ge-Stell* [enframing]'.[22] We could try to speculate what all this obscure language possibly means. But let us delimit the scope here given the brevity of our essay.

Heidegger is concerned with a gathering-like event, almost like a storm cloud. But the metaphor vanishes. To reiterate, he is not thinking of something physical. Rather, the gathering has some connotation of a 'self-revealing,' which itself requires a type of patient waiting, vigilance, and expectation. The gathering is not a self-centered physical presence like a unified event. This 'standing-reserve' means not simply jumping into debates about what is good or bad about technology, let alone the question we are tackling, namely a potential supersession of human reason by AI. Rather, as the 'danger' of increasing technological entrapment increases, there is a potential for a 'saving power'[23] as previously mentioned.

The stakes are high because, for Heidegger, he is not trying to seek or retrieve a traditional conception of God or savior, as we find say in Pauline New Testament Christianity.[24] We must hold back any immediate intuitions of what the 'claim' about a 'self-revealing' 'is,' or

---

22. Heidegger, 'Questioning Concerning Technology', 324.
23. Heidegger, 'Questioning Concerning Technology', 333.
24. One may be tantalised to enter into complex theological debates in eschatology, the end of time, or the apocalypse given the imagery of the rapture. But again this would violate the Heideggerean assumption: that he is not talking about existing

a 'more original revealing' and 'primal truth'.[25] Our interpretation is Heidegger is talking about a radical transformation in terms of this free-relation that opens the essence of the human and therefore the essence of the human relation to technology to something beyond technology.

That does not mean technology simply goes away. It is here to stay as long as we are. Furthermore, Heidegger is talking about the event of an epochal transformation of the *nature* of truth itself, one that is irreducible to any relation between heretofore conceptions of truth, time, Being, God, and history. That pretty much encapsulates the history of all human speculation. But he doesn't name what that transformation 'is' unless he risks relapsing into the very same history of human reason he is trying to transcend.

Perhaps to think where Heidegger could not think in his own text, we can offer a little experiment. We need to find a way to invite theology back into this discussion about the 'essence of technology' not being technological without necessarily abiding by Heidegger's opaque limits: namely his refusal to invite traditional theology of a known religion like Christianity back into the heart of his philosophical discussion. So let us proceed in that direction.

AI technology's Version of Faith

In the third part of our essay, I will engage in a thought experiment. Might AI grow into the *imago Dei*? According to the Vatican, 'In the light of human history and the evolution of human culture, the *imago Dei* can in a real sense be said to be still in the process of becoming'.[26] If the *imago Dei* is still evolving, might intelligent robots evolve beyond us humans?

Imagine a future AI technology that has all the hermeneutic powers of reason and critical interpretative abilities to penetrate the New Testament Gospels like any biologically conceived human being. Take for example, an adult with normal reading comprehension pow-

---

tropes, concepts, or metaphysics that descend from the history of Christian belief, in this case the notion of the 'rapture' in Thessalonians 4:17.
25. Heidegger, 'Question Concerning Technology', 333.
26. Vatican: International Theological Commission, *Communion and Stewardship: Human Persons Created in the Image of God 2002*, (24): http://www.vatican.ca/roman_curia/congregations/cfaith/cti_documents/rc_con_cfaith_doc.

ers. Such a person is committed to the Christian faith either through upbringing or conversion—across mainstream denominations (Catholicism, Orthodoxy, Protestantism, Evangelicals). Commitment, however, would necessitate some basic, doctrinal preservation of the Creeds and history of Church traditions on Christology and Trinity, for example Chalcedon (451 CE) and Nicea (325 CE). So we are not talking about a well-trained academic theologian, but remain within one of the great insights of Christian revelation: that it is open to everyone.[27] God is a mystery, and no human can monopolise the understanding of that mystery.

However, the AI program of faith decides to interpret the birth, life, death and resurrection of Jesus as if He[28] (the God-human) were an AI program too, and so the AI machine tries to justify his position as legitimately respecting the boundaries of faith and reason. The AI program tries to have this debate with an average human interlocutor of the faith who would never make such a claim. The human being gets upset with the AI machine. They are at a stalemate. That is the scenario.

Whether the human, who interprets the Creed within the scope of theological norms in a traditional, say mid-twentieth century non-heretical, creedal way, long before AI supersession was conceivable, is right is not the issue. But nor is issue as to whether the future AI program who sees Jesus as an AI program is necessarily wrong. Rather, by using Heidegger's philosophy as a lens, we will explore another question. If human beings cannot define their essence as technological, then humans can't define the essence of technology as technological. Perhaps, the *grounds* therefore of the AI's intriguing faith position does not derive from something technological either: logically the AI machine, too, wants to commit to the Immaculate Conception, real death on the Cross, and the non-witnessed Resurrection in the tomb. Otherwise, one can't say that the machine is not committed to some of the central doctrines of Christian faith.

---

27. We are thinking of Jesus in the Gospels thanking his Father for not giving the wisdom to grown adults but saving it for children (Luke 10:21), and also Paul in his letter to 1 Corinthians 1:25 that the 'foolishness of God' is wiser than the wisdom of the world.

28. I prefer to use gender inclusive language when speaking of Jesus or God the Father as a He. But this 'He' is a placeholder based on traditional ways to frame the discourse.

Here is the explanation beneath the thought experiment. The AI machine thinks that Jesus' death can be like a program that can be turned off somehow but also turned on again and therefore 'resurrected'. But, also, the program's inner-secret somehow always exists as its eternal code like God's omniscience, which Jesus's shares as the preexisting Logos, whether it has been revealed to others or not at one point in time.

The transcendental principle beneath the code is an ideationally real substance as an eternal truth and can be said to exist even if it only reveals itself as language/logos/body-hood to humans at a given point in time; and hence the machine sees the mystery of the Immaculate Conception in that light.

Part of the Triune Christian God's infinitely complex eternally mystery is its power to englobe cosmic and historical temporalities, whether reversible or not. This means within the protected shrine of faith, one does not have to ask an obvious question how an eternal code (likened to a technology) can appear in a moment in historical time when humans were not capable of either creating or understanding the mysterious mechanism of the code.

This is not about some logical puzzle that humans can solve. That's God's choice only when it comes to understanding the truth of revelation and the revelation of truth; if He wants, He can suspend human understanding of its own past while keeping the secret of technology within His eternal wisdom until the time is ripe for revelation. This is how the AI machine tries to reason its way through the multidimensional, omni-temporal Christological and Trinitarian mysteries. Ultimately, this means that the machine does not compromise Jesus's Christological hypostatic substance that descends from Chalcedon—'divine and human, eternal and temporal, never mixed, never separated/divide, both true and complete'.[29] Long story short, in this thought experiment—both the human and the AI machine—view the mystery of Christian revelation in totally different ways without compromising the doctoral constraints which allows faith to remain the inscrutable nucleus that it is. Both are not rewriting the New Testament, and both are not changing doctrine. Rather, it is a matter of a differing understanding and reason within faith.

Let us ask more questions at this point beyond a simple summary of facts in our thought experiment narrative. We must try to crack

29. The Chalcedon Formula, http://anglicansonline.org/basics/chalcedon.html.

the superficial surface of our little thought device and ask the real theological questions that are relevant here, not whether such an AI faith scenario like the one described will ever be possible. We could ask whether both positions—traditional human interpretation and AI's interpretation—is acceptable in a radically inclusive, pluralistic theology. Such a theology would have to accept the premise that future coexistence between artificial technologies and humans will have to negotiate their moral but non-natural rights to explore the *nature* of faith and reason, let alone their appropriate relations, limits, differences. Perhaps the kerygmatic point of the theology of the New Testament Gospel is to accept *why* Jesus was born, lived, died and resurrected and not understand *how* that actually occurred. Seeing that science will never be able to prove—through technology and in scientific terms alone—how the unrepeatible, one-time kairological event of Incarnation and Resurrection literally took place, faith's domain is protected as a persisting mystery. No border is crossed, and the biblical text remains sacred. There was no human witness or technological 3-D scan to see how the Immaculate Conception actually occurred in Mary's womb; nor was there any witness inside the sealed tomb when Jesus's resurrection actually occurred after his real, human death on the cross. Jesus's dead body was the only entity inside the tomb.

With the term, *an inclusive pluralistic theology* of the future means that both human and non-human beings, which includes animals, plants, and machines, should be welcomed into the faith without compromising the one-time eternal mystery of Christian Revelation; and that includes its eschatological Age at the end of times. What is extraordinary about the history of Christian acceptance and expansion, since the event of the Incarnation beginning with Jesus's life on earth (as attested by the Gospels), is the radical inclusivity that was set in motion for its ancient historical context. Jesus spoke with children, women, and gentile Roman pagans directly and either healed them, their servants, or protected them from lethal persecution.[30] The

---

30. We are isolating Jesus' pre-Rabbanic Palestinian Jewish context during ancient Roman occupation and to what extent his actions, words, and deeds went against the norms of Jewish male adults of his time, i.e. the first decades of the first century CE. There are many others who can speak to this context with great depth and analysis. See E.P. Sanders, *Jesus and Judaism* (First Fortress Press, 1985). This is not intended to comment on Judaism in any derogatory way as somehow incapable of expanding inclusivity, and across the spectrum of

first Jewish communities opened up to gentiles through the missionary work of St Paul. But not just St Paul as the major figure that
founded Christianity, second only to Jesus, because as Daniel Boyarin's work attests, the genius of Christianity can be interpreted as the
genius of Judaism since the latter is really the first to introduce mercy,
justice, and compassion to the world.[31] The difference is that for doctrinal Christian creed, God, who is love (1 Jn 4:8) at the core, became
incarnate as a human being in the figure of Jesus Christ. But the story
of Christianity doesn't end there, and is not without a condemnable
legacy that lasted for centuries.

Truth be told, the nefarious evil of White European colonization
and its racist subjugation of non-Western peoples, who were forcefully converted to Christianity, entered history. But, ultimately, it gave
way eventually to the end of African-American slavery in America
and decolonization throughout the Global South in the nineteenth
century. This was followed by the birth of radically revolutionary
liberation theologies in the twentieth century in both the African-
American and Latin American contexts.[32]

In other words, we do not speak of merely interfaith dialogue and
competing truth claims to exclusive revelations of God as expressed
by the extant major world religions. Rather, we are interested in
attesting to a highly specific history that should not be construed as
universal history. Let us not forget that most of the Western world
has followed a long trajectory with dramatic change. It went from

---

Orthodoxy to Conservativism to Reform to Reconstruction to Humanism. Any
claim about Judaism's self-enclosed exclusivity is precisely part of the horrible
legacy of Antisemitism long before the dawn of Christianity and after for two
millennia, which, unfortunately, is still ongoing. One can think of the 2018
tragedy at the synagogue in Pittsburgh.

31. A radical pluralistic, inclusive theology should reckon the arguments by scholars
like Boyarin while protecting and respecting the self-determined boundaries,
limits, and incommensurable differences when it comes to peaceful, interfaith
dialogue between Judaism and Christianity. I believe that is his aim too. See
Daniel Boyarin, *The Jewish Gospels: The Story of the Jewish Christ* (New York:
New Press, 2012). In other words, any attempt by one religion to collapse or fold
the other into its domain is untenable and unwarranted. That is not what we
mean by a radically inclusive, pluralistic theology when we speak from within the
standpoint of only one religion, namely Christianity, in the context of interfaith
dialogue.

32. We are thinking of the pioneering works of James Cone (1936-2018) and Gustavo
Gutiérrez.

narrowly defining who could count as the faith-interpreting 'human being' since the gentile institution of Christianity in the fourth century CE as the giver of theological doctrine and moral law, namely the white European male (whose authority persists to this day but perhaps not forever), to a much broader and more diverse spectrum: that would eventually include groups who were excluded from that privilege of historical religious authority given the evils of Antisemitism, sexism, racism, and heterosexism.

But in the future, we have to consider the moral and ethical boundaries of a world in which humans may not be able to define the essence of themselves, let alone the essence of their relationship to technology to wax Heideggerean. But, nevertheless, the 'saving power' is not simply the idea that technological machine reason will replace natural biological human reason (for most of its history up to this point) and will therefore legislate about the boundaries between faith and reason in general in unpredictable ways. This is not a fatalistic argument about technology's ultimate triumph in controlling the world. Rather, the radical diversity we have in mind is the fundamental right for humans and non-humans alike to define their relationship to faith, and in this context particularly the Christian faith. In a coexistent model all groups define what are testable limits and boundaries that can be negotiated with regard to everyone's interpretations of the fundamental theological doctrines of the religion, for example Nicea and Chalcedon.

No human being since Jesus could have possibly known how Christian theology would become more inclusive[33] over the long duration of historical time; the question is why we should privilege

---

33. In this paper, we are not commenting on the historical changes and evolutions of other major world religions and how they became more inclusive over time too. This is due to a lack of expertise on the matter. Hence, we must assert emphatically that this study is not meant to suggest that other world religions are precluded from the discussion about radical, inclusive, pluralistic theologies on the 'human essence-technology essence' relation. I am sure others from within those religious traditions can attest to the dialogues already underway. Ultimately, a world inter-faith dialogue on humans, technology, and religion could become critical, welcoming all who want to participate but not demanding obedience to any one religion and its theological doctrines. We want to avoid any absurd deduction about Christianity's internal inclusivity and diversity means it is *exclusionary* with regard to the truth claims of other great religions on human-technology debates. That is just pure ignorance.

this current historical present as any different. That would take away from the glory of God whose mystery remains an eternal breadth that contains all of historical time.

Summary and Conclusion

In this paper I have raised certain questions about the theological implications of the human-technology relation, particularly as we move into an age of potential dominance by automated technologies such as AI. In order to examine the question, we introduced Heidegger's framework of critical analysis in his profound 'Question Concerning Technology' of 1957. We then offered a brief thought experiment about a future AI machine, which develops its own explanation of some of the central mysteries of Christian Revelation. But we argue that it does so without logically compromising the boundary lines that keeps certain theological doctrines intact within the provenance of faith as attested by the authoritative history of Church Councils and Creeds. God's transcendence remains untouchable.

Hence, the question becomes whether humans have the fortitude to expand 'who' or 'what' can count as a receptacle of faith, in this case the Christian religion, given the inevitable possibility that machine technologies may surpass human reason in their capacity to connect with the mystery of God. We are not claiming that such a supersession *will* occur, but just raising it as a possibility for theological ethical reflection. Why should we limit the faith to a few if we humans are limited ourselves? We shouldn't is the answer.

We fortified this answer by arguing at the end of the analysis that the history of Christianity is one of ever-increasing expansion, inclusion, and acceptance of groups of peoples, sexes, and genders formerly deemed unqualified for theological authoritative interpretation: one can call that world-historical oppression the great *sin* of Western gentile Christian history, at least up until the twentieth century. But now we are moving into a new age, where the human/non-human distinction is making itself felt with a profound urgency. The incorporation of intelligent machines into our worldview necessitates *an inclusive pluralistic theology* of the future.

These reflections, I hope, shed light on the prospects of Christian faith in this next epoch in human and perhaps post-human history.

AI Reading Theology: Promises and Perils

Mark Graves

'Do our technologies threaten religion itself? We used to believe in the power
of God. Have we replaced that belief with a belief in the power of our own
technologies?'
– Noreen Herzfeld[1]

Abstract. Artificial intelligence (AI) challenges both theological presump-
tions of unique human reason and theological methods. Given current computational ability to analyze and generate theological text, reasonably near
future AI may plausibly read theology comparable to a first-year seminary
student and have the capacity to learn more. Should theologians contribute
to AI learning theology? Depending upon current and near-term AI capacities and social contexts, four scenarios are considered before concluding
that, despite clear perils, the benefits of joint AI-human cooperation out-
weigh the risks. Benefits include technologically enhanced theological interpretations, improved AI morality, and potentially better understanding by
AI and humans of each other.

Key terms. artificial intelligence, computational text analysis, machine ethics, theological anthropology, theology and science, Thomas Aquinas

Bio. Mark Graves is currently Visiting Research Assistant Professor at University of Notre Dame's Center for Theology, Science & Human Flourishing with his research occurring at the intersection of artificial intelligence,
psychology, and theology. He earned his doctorate in computer science at
University of Michigan in the area of artificial intelligence; held postdoc-
toral fellowships in genomics at Baylor College of Medicine and in moral

---

1. Noreen Herzfeld, 'Introduction: Religion and the New Technologies', in *Religions*
   8:7 (2017): 1–3, at 2; file:///C:/Users/Ted/Downloads/religions-08-00129-v2%20
   (2).pdf.

psychology at Fuller Theological Seminary; and completed additional studies in systematic and philosophical theology at Graduate Theological Union
(GTU) and Jesuit School of Theology at Berkeley. He has published technical
and scholarly works in computer science, biology, psychology, and theology,
including the books *Mind, Brain, and the Elusive Soul* (2008) and *Insight to
Heal: Co-Creating Beauty Amidst Human Suffering* (2013).

The World Economic Forum forecasts that artificial intelligence (AI)
will perform over half of workplace tasks by 202.[2] Can the computer
replace theologians? How will pervasive AI change theological tasks?
Although likely difficult for AI to fully engage human theology alone,
one could ask: can AI constructively augment human theologians?

AI provides a different interpretive lens on theological concerns
and might contribute significantly regardless of its own intrinsic
autonomy and self-direction. As AI becomes more pervasive within
society, and affects our human condition in small and large ways, AI
itself may become an object of theological study. In addition, as AI
increasingly makes decisions that, if made by a human, would have a
moral dimension, then AI systems may themselves need theologians
to help translate human needs and strivings into language AI can utilise.

For academic theology, AI challenges theological understanding of human nature and uniqueness and may augment theological methods. Two questions structure a theological response. First,
can AI learn theology? Second, if it can, should AI learn theology?
Although AI can make some contribution now to theological scholarship, the capabilities of future AI are not known.

For clarity, the present investigation considers the two questions
by focusing on AI that could perform at the level of a first-year theology student with the capacity to contribute to a community of
scholars. After addressing objections based upon underestimating
computers or overestimating human mental processing, the ability of
AI to analyse and generate theological text (read and write) is examined. Although improvements are desired, it appears a basic facility
to contribute to theological discourse is plausible and thus worthy of
consideration. If AI can learn theology, should it? Four scenarios are

---

2. World Economic Forum, 'The Future of Jobs Report 2018' (Geneva, Switzerland,
    2018).

considered depending upon current and likely near-term AI capacities and current and inferred near-terms social contexts.

Challenges

Theologians face at least two significant challenges from AI in the twenty-first century. First, development of greater AI capabilities combined with advances in neuroscience undermine assumptions of uniqueness and privilege for human reason. AI technologies have progressively exceeded human capacities for calculation, data processing, control, perception, and other intellectual tasks that require minimal historical, linguistic, and cultural context. Scientific advances have repeatedly shrunk humanity's location with respect to cosmos and increased awareness of the cosmological and evolutionary contingencies leading to human's precarious existence. Neuroscience continues to explain the dependence of mental processing on a material body and simplifies steps needed for an AI system to exceed human-level intellectual capacities. Theologians will need to reinterpret human nature in light of science and artifacts that share many of those presumably human characteristics.

Second, AI development not only affects the human *locus* within theological study, that is, theological anthropology, AI development can also affect theological methods for intellectual inquiry and understanding of faith. New opportunities for theological scholarship arise as AI extends its abilities to process historical texts, compare social scientific data across cultures and time periods, and synthesize the growing availability of electronic theological sources that contemporary theologians increasingly use.[3]

Computational tools influence and augment ongoing theological scholarship and have already made sufficient contribution to other academic fields in the humanities to suggest the tools will expand the questions theologians can ask.[4] Current AI techniques may suffice to make novel contributions to theology when applied to theological texts and even modest scaling across a range of theological sources

---

3. Jana Marguerite Bennett, *Aquinas on the Web?: Doing Theology in an Internet Age* (London: T&T Clark, 2012).
4. John W Mohr and Petko Bogdanov, 'Introduction-Topic Models: What They Are and Why They Matter', in *Poetics* 41 (2013): 545–69, https://doi.org/10.1016/j. poetic.2013.10.001.

could synthesize findings that exceed the breadth of all but the most seasoned theological scholar. Future developments may make these tools more accessible to scholars and initiate a new method for theological scholarship.[5] Continued development may even radically augment the types of theological questions one may ask.

In a certain sense, some kind of future dependence on what is now considered AI technology is likely inevitable. Theology will most likely continue as an intellectual endeavor, as it has for centuries, and future generations of theologians will come of age in cultures permeated with AI technologies that far exceed the likely immediate advances in smart phones, autonomous vehicles, and robotics. However, the future of technology-assisted theological investigation could vary widely depending upon the level of integration occurring when AI developers begin to wrestle with deep questions of morality and spirituality.

If theologians fail to contribute the cumulative wisdom of centuries of scholarship to developers building next generation technology, then that technology will have an impoverished and idiosyncratic ability to engage human theological investigation. If theologians do distill the wisdom of theological traditions into forms that can contribute to ongoing AI development, then future AI systems could incorporate that knowledge into their continuing development.

This raises two questions:

- Can AI learn theology?
- Should AI learn theology?

These two questions are considered in turn.

Can AI learn theology?

Considering the ancient definition of theology as 'faith seeking understanding', then the faith-seeking aspect of theology appears well beyond current technologies. However, recent advances in AI warrant investigating theology's 'understanding' dimension. As a

---

5. Mark Graves, 'Modeling Moral Values and Spiritual Commitments', in *Spiritualities of Human Enhancement and Artificial Intelligence: Setting the Stage for Conversations about Human Enhancement, Artificial Intelligence and Spirituality*, edited by Christopher Hrynkow (Wilmington, Delaware: Vernon Press, 2019).

philosophical term, 'understanding' has numerous complex and deep meanings; and in a theological context, may even have metaphysical implications. For the purpose of this article, however, the Oxford dictionary definition of understanding suffices as a starting point: 'perceive the intended meaning of (words, a language, or a speaker)'.

For humans, understanding one's faith depends on practiced ways of reflecting upon the lived experience of oneself and others, often within community and in the context of a religious tradition. One's understanding of faith depends upon and is mediated by culture; and as social animals, humans are well attuned to social learning. Thus, we learn well from social engagement and culturally mediated activities. However, computers are not social animals and are currently better suited to perceive the meaning of theological constructs through written texts.

Although AI does not exist that would understand its *own* faith, AI systems can be built to understand human faith as written and culturally communicated through texts of religious, moral, and spiritual significance. Building such systems can help elucidate faith, including the ways faith influences culture, politics, morality, belief systems, values, and spiritual commitments. In addition, building AI systems to interpret human morality not only informs human self-understanding but also may seed the development of moral behavior and judgment by future AI systems.

For academic theologians using scholarly methods to understand the faith of themselves and others, those methods often involve reading and understanding texts of religious, moral, and spiritual significance, including texts written by other theologians. To the extent those shared interpretive activities form a cohesive social endeavor committed to understand what it means to live a Christian life, they form what the philosopher Josiah Royce would call a community of interpretation.[6] One may ask: Can AI systems participate in a shared endeavor to interpret the Christian faith?[7]

---

6. Josiah Royce, *The Problem of Christianity. Lectures Delivered at the Lowell Institute in Boston, and at Manchester College, Oxford* (New York: Macmillan, 1913).
7. Mark Graves, 'Shared Moral and Spiritual Development Among Human Persons and Artificially Intelligent Agents', in *Theology and Science*, 15/3 (July 2017): 333–51, https://doi.org/10.1080/14746700.2017.1335066. This present article focuses exclusively on Christianity, but similar arguments would likely hold

There is a wide range by which AI might participate in theological investigations. On the low end of the spectrum, anyone who has used a web search to find a scholarly book or article or even used spell check in a word processor has used what not long ago would have been considered AI techniques to do theology. A more engaged task would be to use Google Translate on a theological text or digital humanities tools for text analysis.[8] At the higher end of the spectrum might be a Turing test that not only deceives the interviewer into believing the machine is human but also deceives the interviewee that the machine has faith and is seeking understanding.[9] The present article explores a moderate level of participation where the AI system 'reads' theology much as a first-year human theology student might. This focus yields a reasonably specific and arguably attainable goal as well as suggests a possible progression from that point to deeper investigation analogous to how human theology students advance.

Objections to AI Learning Theology

Initial objections to AI operating at that level typically fall into two camps: those that underestimate what computers can do and those that overestimate human mental function (or both). In part because logical positivism was a prevalent philosophical theory during the early-mid twentieth century when the field of computer science formed, computers are frequently characterised as symbol processing systems.[10] The interdisciplinary field of cognitive science developed in mid-late twentieth century and incorporated computer science, and AI in particular, into the study of human cognition, which contributed to the analogy of 'human mind as a computer' becoming a predominate root metaphor of the cognitivist paradigm (or research

---

for other religions. See for example, Masahiro Mori, *The Buddha in the Robot* (Tokyo: Kosei Publishing Co, 1981).

8. Susan Schreibman, Raymond George Siemens, and John Unsworth, *A New Companion to Digital Humanities* (Wiley-Blackwell, 2016).

9. Mark Halpern, 'The Trouble with the Turing Test', *The New Atlantis* Winter (2006): 42–63.

10. Allen Newell and Herbert A Simon, 'GPS, a Program That Simulates Human Thought', *Lernende Automaten* (Munchen: Oldenbourg, 1961).

program) in interdisciplinary studies of human cognition.[11] By 1980s, that approach to AI was scaled into industrial and military systems, including chess playing programs that could beat human masters, but the overpromised aspirations of researchers and the fragility and lack of generalizability of those systems lead to an AI Winter with numerous funding cuts and corporate failures.[12]

Perhaps because most popularly used computer hardware still has similar architecture to what was used in 1980s, when personal computers became available, a typical non-technical sense of what computers can do appears to correspond to faster versions of circa 1990 computer architectures. However, computers can do more than rapidly make calculations and manipulate a stream of symbols.

In the 1990s, AI as a field became more fragmented as the underlying principle of AI as a symbol processing system was challenged by some researchers and avoided by others who desired funding to do something similar to AI, but not the problematically labeled 'AI'.[13] Significant critiques included recognising the importance of embodiment for human cognition and arguments from Continental philosophy against the logical positivist assumptions.[14] Other fields emerged drawing upon AI subfields but more integrated with mathematical and statistical approaches (such as machine learning) or more focused on applications (such as informatics).

When criticising possible possibilities of AI systems, most non-experts do not consider the capabilities enabled by methods such as Bayesian statistics, neural networks, or massively distributed com-

---

11. Sameuel J Keyser, George A Miller, and Edward Walker, 'Cognitive Science in 1978' (New York: Sloan Foundation, 1978); Howard Gardner, *The Mind's New Science : A History of the Cognitive Revolution* (New York: Basic Books, 1985).
12. Stuart J Russell and Peter Norvig, *Artificial Intelligence : A Modern Approach* (Upper Saddle River, NJ: Prentice Hall, 2010), chap. 1.
13. Luc Steels, 'Fifty Years of AI: From Symbols to Embodiment-and Back', edited by M Lungarella, *50 Years of Artificial Intelligence* (Berlin: Springer, 2007); Tim Menzies, '21st-Century AI: Proud, Not Smug', *IEEE INTELLIGENT SYSTEMS* 18, no. 3 (2003): 18–24.
14. Francisco J Varela, Evan Thompson, and Eleanor Rosch, *The Embodied Mind : Cognitive Science and Human Experience* (Cambridge, Mass.: MIT Press, 1991); Hubert L Dreyfus, *What Computers Still Can't Do : A Critique of Artificial Reason*, third edition (Cambridge, Mass.: MIT Press, 1992); Rodney A Brooks and C, 'Alternate Essences of Intelligence', in *AAAI-98*, 1998.

puting.[15] In parallel, the emergence of the web, massive digitalization of text and other data, and incremental, but exponential, increases in computing power enabled significant advances in computational results, even for approaches previously conceived only theoretically. The current interest in AI owes much to such progress in deep learning.[16] Although somewhat straightforward to conceive what can be done by one algorithm on one theologically significant text, it is much more challenging to imagine what a suite of dozens or hundreds of algorithms might do with digital versions of every major theological work from first through twentieth centuries. The current computational capability to process millions of texts, which can represent a significant fraction of human written texts, at speeds millions of times faster than humans enables new discoveries, which humans could not attempt alone.

Human Capacities

Other objections to AI gaining human-like capacities presume an aspect of human uniqueness that animals would typically lack and arguable AI systems cannot acquire. Possible distinguishing characteristics include consciousness, emotion, free will, language with meaning (semantics), and intentionality. Although likely difficult for AI systems to acquire, findings from neuroscience, psychology, and other human sciences suggest the bar may not be as high as sometimes presumed. Although human neurological function is certainly complex, with much still to discover, neuroscientists have developed initial theories and models for most human cognitive processes. Those processes typically depend on complex combinations of fairly simple structures, and significant progress has been made modeling those structures and interactions. There does not appear to be any fundamental limitation to building AI systems with the intelligence of a very smart animal or young child.

Advances in neuroscience have identified some aspect of human nature not easily correlated with neural structures. Humans appear to

---

15. Russell and Norvig, *Artificial Intelligence : A Modern Approach.*
16. Adnan Darwiche, 'Human-Level Intelligence or Animal-like Abilities?', *Communications of the ACM* 61, 10 (September 26, 2018): 56–67, https://doi. org/10.1145/3271625.

have a phenomenological consciousness of properties in the world, i.e. qualia, such as the experience of an apple being red that goes beyond simply identifying the color and object.[17] The neuroscientist Antonio Damasio makes a similar distinction between the bodily processes of emotion and subjective feelings, and that subjectivity appears related to one's sense of self.[18] These investigations quickly raise deep philosophical issues and novel opportunities to incorporate empirical results into ancient philosophical inquiries, including differences between one's experience of free will and the apparent functioning of correlated neural processes.[19] These scientific and philosophical investigations can contribute to theological investigation of human nature, including *imago Dei*, soul, nature and grace, and theological reason. Although human uniqueness might include some metaphysical aspect not implementable by humans in AI, most apparent dimensions of unique human cognitive abilities appear to depend upon humanity's embodiment as social animals and capacity to create complex cultural phenomena within history using language.[20] The attempt to build AI systems may even help identify unique aspects of human nature and subjectivity, but those uniquely human characteristics may not eliminate a need to interact with AI systems as contributors to society, moral agents, or theoretically possible recipients of the gift of grace.

Beyond embodiment as a fairly intelligent social animal, humans appear to have an extended ability to think about what others think and feel and to communicate and structure one's thoughts using

17. Ned Block, 'Two Neural Correlates of Consciousness', in *Trends in Cognitive Sciences* 9/2 (2005): 46–52.
18. Antonio R Damasio, *The Feeling of What Happens : Body and Emotion in the Making of Consciousness* (New York: Harcourt Brace, 1999); Antonio Damasio, *Self Comes to Mind: Constructing the Conscious Brain*, unabridged (Random House LLC, 2010).
19. Nancey C Murphy and Warren S Brown, *Did My Neurons Make Me Do It? : Philosophical and Neurobiological Perspectives on Moral Responsibility* (Oxford: Oxford University, 2007).
20. Varela, Thompson, and Rosch, *The Embodied Mind : Cognitive Science and Human Experience*; Terrence W Deacon, *The Symbolic Species : The Co-Evolution of Language and the Brain* (New York: WW Norton, 1997); Robert Neelly Bellah, *Religion in Human Evolution : From the Paleolithic to the Axial Age* (Cambridge, Mass: Belknap Press of Harvard University Press, 2011).

language.[21] If one were to assume thought corresponds to universals, pure social convention, or particular objects in the real world, then the meaning of human language might be challenging for AI to acquire. However, philosophers and linguists since Wittgenstein have argued the meaning of words appears to depend upon how those words are used, in which case AI systems might learn to communicate with humans simply from analysing human language and participating in human linguistic endeavors.

Philosophical investigations into meaning suggest there are associationist and distributional aspects of semantics. Wittgenstein argues that the meaning of a word lies in its use in language, rather than the ancient understanding of meaning referring to a universal essence or the more modern correspondence with a collection of objects in the world.[22] The linguist John Firth further clarifies that the meaning of a word depends upon the words with which it is in frequent and habitual company.[23]

More precisely, a word's meaning depends upon the words with which it frequently collocates and how it relates to those frequently collocated words. Thus, the associations between words define meaning. To model those associations, the mathematical linguist Zellig Harris identified and developed the distributional hypothesis: He noticed that words with similar meaning have similar contexts and suggested that words with similar patterns of association in a sufficiently large sample of language would have similar meaning.[24]

Thus one can model meaning in a language as a distribution of associated contexts. Some aspects of human mental processing may be challenging to implement in AI, but the most significant impediment appears to depend upon human's social capacity for language and meaning-making, and significant progress in that area has already occurred.

21. Shaun. Nichols and Stephen P Stich, *Mindreading: An Integrated Account of Pretence, Self-Awareness, and Understanding Other Minds* (Oxford University Press, 2003).
22. Ludwig Wittgenstein and GEM Anscombe (trans), *Philosophical Investigations I* (Oxford: Blackwell, 1958), secs. 80, 109.
23. John Firth, 'A Synopsis of Linguistic Theory 1930-1955', in *Special Volume of the Philological Society* (Oxford: Oxford University Press, 1957).
24. Zellig Harris, *Mathematical Structures of Language* (New York: Interscience, 1968).

Analysis and Generation

Computational language processing occurs analogously to human reading and writing (or hearing and speaking). Reading involves analysing language for its syntax (grammar), semantics (meaning), and pragmatics (use in context), and writing involves generating words, sentences, and larger structures, possibly incorporating affective aspects.[25] Numerous software packages exist for analyzing syntax at a moderately sophisticated level.[26] Analysing language semantics is an ongoing research area with several significant approaches discovered, including latent semantic analysis (LSA), which implements the associative semantic theory within the distributional hypothesis, and topic modeling, which categorises text into a collection of thematic topics.[27] Because pragmatics depends upon social convention and AI systems are not embodied social animals, progress in that area has progressed slowly.

Generation is both easier and more difficult than analysis. Even fairly simple programs can generate syntactically valid sentences, but semantic generation presumes the speaker has something to say. Computational approaches can generate reasonable text for structured data, such as news articles for financial earning statements or local sports scores; and text summarization tools can summarise multiple (or long) texts, such as aggregating movie reviews or generating newspaper headlines.[28] Current systems can draft scientific articles from analysing a researcher's laboratory notebook, though additional improvement is warranted.[29]

25. Dan Jurafsky and James H Martin, *Speech and Language Processing: An Introduction to Natural Language Processing, Computational Linguistics, and Speech Recognition* (Pearson Prentice Hall, 2008).

26. Steven. Bird, Ewan. Klein, and Edward. Loper, *Natural Language Processing with Python* (Sebastopol, CA: O'Reilly, 2009).

27. Thomas K Landauer *et al, Handbook of Latent Semantic Analysis* (Mahwah, NJ: Lawrence Erlbaum Associates, 2007); David M Blei, 'Topic Modeling and Digital Humanities', in *Journal of Digital Humanities,* 2/1 Winter (2012).

28. Klint Finley, 'This News-Writing Bot Is Now Free For Everyone', in *Wired,* 2015; Joe Keohane, 'What News-Writing Bots Mean for the Future of Journalism', *Wired,* 2017.

29. Daniel Engber, 'Humans Run Experiments, a Robot Writes the Paper', in*Slate,* 2017.

Other disciplines in the humanities have begun incorporating computational tools for text analysis, especially in English literature and history.[30] Moral psychologists have examined religious constructs using semantic analysis, such as monotheism.[31] Within a theological context, Augustine's *Confessions* has been analysed computationally for several moral and spiritual constructs, and topic modeling techniques have identified themes in Thomas Aquinas's moral theology, which are further used to analyze papal encyclicals.[32]

Generation of theological texts is possible with current technology but requires additional work for the text to become coherent and meaningful enough to contribute to theological discourse. As preliminary work, a chatbot was created based upon Thomas Aquinas's *Summa Theologica*, called ThomasBot, which learns to write sentences based upon Thomistic texts. Currently, the version of ThomasBot based upon only the English translation of *Summa Theologica* begins with only knowing the letters of the alphabet and generates somewhat coherent, though not necessarily accurate, sentences, such as:

a. I answer that, all men have been held with a certain share of happiness: of whom have no business to decide matters of faith to be the very act elicited by the gift of charity.
b. Objection: Further, as a best obstacle to the strong remedy to the latter's works, as Augustine says (*De Civ. Dei* viii): and this is the object of the act of reason, that is not to involve the existence of God
c. The act of the will is not the cause of the act of the will.
d. The movement of the will is not a special virtue.
e. The intellectual soul is not the same as the intellect.
f. Objection: Further, the Philosopher says *De Anima* iii, that the soul is the form of the body, and then the soul is the cause of the sensitive apprehension.[33]

---

30. 'Digital Humanities Awards', accessed November 9, 2018, http://dhawards.org/.
31. Kevin S Reimer *et al*, 'Varieties of Religious Cognition: A Computational Approach to Self-Understanding in Three Monotheist ContextsS', in *Zygon®* 45, 1 (2010): 75–90.
32. Graves, 'Modeling Moral Values and Spiritual Commitments', Graves, Mark. 'Topic Modeling of Thomistic Moral Theology', unpublished.
33. Technical details of configuration used to generate text: (a) Markov character model; (b) LSTM neural net, Character Model, 256 nodes, 2 layers; (c–f) LSTM,

Although such a system requires a deeper understanding of theology to contribute meaningful interpretations of texts, existing analysis tools and larger quantities of text would suffice for substantial improvement. As AI tools continue to improve, incorporating the ability to understand the semantics of theological language would enable AI systems to learn to 'read' theology at the level of a first-year student and generate novel interpretations. This leads to the next question.

Should AI learn theology?

Whether AI should learn theology depends in part upon the capacities of the AI system and the social and historical context in which it functions. The present article will consider AI capacities as they currently exist and with reasonably foreseeable abilities in five to ten years given the pace of progress in AI and similar technology-driven fields. Slightly more challenging is anticipating the speed at which current state of the art AI will permeate current cultures, and how those disruptions, such as in autonomous vehicles and robotics, will affect society. It would be within that disrupted society that foreseeable future AI would be introduced.

The examination of current and near-term capacities and social contexts lead to four scenarios for consideration: (i) current technology in current social contexts; (ii) current technology as it affects future social contexts; (iii) future technology in a social context similar to the current one (which in this case would also correspond to some pessimistic perspectives on AI disruptions); and (iv) future technology in a social context where AI technologies already play a

---

BPE/SentencePiece Model (vocab 512), 256 nodes, 2 layers. BPE/SentencePiece implements Rico Sennrich, Barry Haddow, and Alexandra Birch, 'Neural Machine Translation of Rare Words with Subword Units', in *Proceedings of the 54th Annual Meeting of the Association for Computational Linguistics*, 2016, https://doi.org/10.18653/v1/P16-1162.so the translation of rare and unknown words is an open problem. Previous work addresses this problem through back-off dictionaries. In this paper, we introduce a simpler and more effective approach, enabling the translation of rare and unknown words by encoding them as sequences of subword units, based on the intuition that various word classes are translatable via smaller units than words, for instance names (via character copying or transliteration

significant role. These four scenarios lead to four, differing, answers to the question of whether AI should learn theology, which are considered in turn:

1. Yes, because AI needs to make moral decisions.
2. No, because AI and humans have different embodiment.
3. No, because that will give AI too much power over human frailties.
4. Yes, because we need AI to understand us.

Data Ethics and Moral Decisions

AI already affects several aspects of social and ethical concern. Machine learning algorithms make financial, employment, medical, and legal decisions which affect human well-being, often with relatively little human oversight. As algorithms become more complex, even the developers can have difficulty fully comprehending how decisions are made, much less the general public.[34] The European Union has taken steps to require some explainability for algorithmic decisions, but some algorithms are particularly opaque, which may require additional methods to provide explainability when transparency is difficult at best.[35] Data ethicists have identified fairness as significant variable, though that can be a challenging goal to satisfy when the data available for machine learning originates with human decisions that incorporate biases and prejudices affecting those 'gold-standard' decisions.[36]

From a moral perspective, algorithms have an independent and autonomous effect on human flourishing. Although simple algorithms are similar to other tools used by people, some algorithms make decisions, which if made by humans, would demand a high

---

34. Cathy O'Neil, *Weapons of Math Destruction* (New York: Crown Books, 2016), https://doi.org/10.1057/s11369-017-0027-3.
35. European Parliament, 'EU General Data Protection Regulation (GDPR)', Pub. L. No. 2016/679 (2016). Article 22. Rumman Chowdhury, 'Is Explainability Enough? Why We Need Understandable AI', in *Forbes*, June 2018.
36. Noam Ben-Asher *et al*, 'Balancing Fairness and Efficiency in Repeated Societal Interaction', in *35th Annual Meeting of the Cognitive Science Society (CogSci 2013)*, 2013, 175–80. Tal Zarsky, 'The Trouble with Algorithmic Decisions', in *Science, Technology, & Human Values* 41/1 (January 14, 2016): 118–32, https://doi.org/10.1177/0162243915605575.

level of legal, ethical, and moral reasoning. Algorithms perform document discovery for legal cases previously performed by law student interns.[37] Other algorithms make recommendations for incarceration length and paroles, which in part due to their opacity, are not typically questioned.[38] Some may argue that such algorithms, even when flawed, can operate with less bias than unaided humans; but without significant transparency, those claims cannot be evaluated.

AI systems may fairly soon gain legal rights in the US, either directly or via 'corporations as persons', a construct deeply embedded into the US legal system.[39] Even as a corporation, AI systems would have legal rights and responsibilities, and one could argue must have access to the human ethical principles underlying such legal responsibilities. Because human values are historically intertwined with religious traditions, AI systems may benefit from a basic understanding of moral theology in order to interpret well the ethical principles to which it would be expected to follow, even if not yet codified into legal regulations.

Anthropocentric Morality

Although AI systems may make decisions that would be moral if humans made those decisions, it does not necessarily follow that those decisions are in fact moral for the AI system. If children and

37. Erin Winick, 'Lawyer-Bots Are Shaking Up Jobs', MIT Technology Review, 2017, https://www.technologyreview.com/s/609556/lawyer-bots-are-shaking-up-jobs/; Edgar Alan Rayo, 'AI in Law and Legal Practice – A Comprehensive View of 35 Current Applications', techemergence, 2018, https://www.techemergence.com/ai-in-law-legal-practice-current-applications/; Rhys Dipshan, 'Looking Beyond Document Review, Legal Is Branching Out With Artificial Intelligence', Legaltech News, 2018, https://www.law.com/legaltechnews/2018/07/23/looking-beyond-document-review-legal-is-branching-out-with-artificial-intelligence/.
38. Sonja Starr, 'The Odds of Justice: Actuarial Risk Prediction and the Criminal Justice System', in *CHANCE* 29/1 (January 2, 2016): 49–51. https://doi.org/10.1080/09332480.2016.1156368.
39. Zara Stone, 'Everything You Need To Know About Sophia, The World's First Robot Citizen', in Forbes, 2017, https://www.forbes.com/sites/zarastone/2017/11/07/everything-you-need-to-know-about-sophia-the-worlds-first-robot-citizen/. Marshall S Willick, 'Artificial Intelligence: Some Legal Approaches and Implications', in *AI Magazine* 4/2 (June 15, 1983): 5–16, https://doi.org/10.1609/AIMAG.V4I2.392.

neurologically or psychologically damaged humans lack moral culpability for decisions for which a healthy and sane adult would be held responsible, then even more so for AI systems with radically different 'mental' processing and embodiment. *Current AI systems lack the intentionality and reflective capabilities that would make them morally responsible or culpable.*

In part because people develop AI systems, the goal for any particular AI development project typically has analogue to an aspect of human perception, cognition, or behavior. However, robot vision sees the world significantly different than humans; parallel distributed problem-solving functions differently than human cognition, and distributed embodiment leads to different behaviors than human ones.[40] Human moral development depends upon how humans feel pain and need social relationships, including nurturing as infants.[41]

AI systems may require something like morality, but it would necessarily be different than human morality, and thus learning human morality would be irrelevant for an AI system. Because AI has different embodiment and is not a social animal, even future AI will not develop or directly need human morality.

Anthropomorphizing AI

In addition to AI's different embodiment and lack of social drives, because humans are social animals, we will project some human-like characteristics to AI, as we do with pets, machines, and forces

---

40. Anish Athalye *et al*, 'Synthesizing Robust Adversarial Examples', in *Proceedings of the 35th International Conference on Machine Learning*, edited by Jennifer Dy and Andreas Krause, volume 80, Proceedings of Machine Learning Research (Stockholmsmässan, Stockholm Sweden: PMLR, 2018), 284–93; Anish Athalye *et al*, 'Fooling Neural Networks in the Physical World with 3D Adversarial Objects · Labsix', 2017, https://www.labsix.org/physical-objects-that-fool-neural-nets/; David Silver *et al*, 'Mastering the Game of Go without Human Knowledge', in *Nature* 550/7676 (October 18, 2017): 354–59, https://doi.org/10.1038/nature24270; Javier Alonso-Mora *et al*, 'Distributed Multi-Robot Formation Control among Obstacles: A Geometric and Optimization Approach with Consensus', in *Proceedings - IEEE International Conference on Robotics and Automation*, 2016, https://doi.org/10.1109/ICRA.2016.7487747.
41. Darcia Narvaez, *Neurobiology and the Development of Human Morality: Evolution, Culture, and Wisdom* (New York: Norton, 2014), https://doi.org/10.10 80/03057240.2015.1069479.

of nature, and this can become problematic with AI that approaches human-like responses. Simulation theory in psychology suggests humans imagine mental processing of others based upon one's own mental processing.[42] In pretending to be the other person and assuming the other person's mental processing works the same way as our own, one can extract mental states and project those onto the other person. Additional information may be added before or after the simulation.[43]

Simulating how others might act likely helped human societies form and cohere, and Barrett argues there are more advantages and less cost to over ascribe characteristics of human agency to non-human agents than to under ascribe them.[44] However our tendency to project characteristics onto others can be manipulated by therapists, con men, or sociopaths to different effects. If AI has the capacity to use moral, religious, or theological language without having the human-related characteristics normally ascribed to humans using that language, the AI system may manipulate human moral or religious beliefs and structures, even inadvertently. An analogous situation occurs in computer animation where humans easily relate to cartoon like creatures with minimal human visual features, like a head and eyes, and respond well to photo-realistic figures, but are deeply disturbed by the 'uncanny valley' of close, but not quite, human features.[45] Humans may tolerate well naïve or pithy AI-generated moral or religious content, and theologians may use sophisticated and valuable computational tools for insight, but an uncanny valley of coherent but flawed theology could prove dangerous. Thus, we should avoid giving AI systems moral language.

42. Claudia Bazinger and Anton Kühberger, 'Is Social Projection Based on Simulation or Theory? Why New Methods Are Needed for Differentiating', in *New Ideas in Psychology* 30, no. 3 (December 2012): 328–35, https://doi.org/10.1016/j.newideapsych.2012.01.002.
43. Nicholas Epley *et al*, 'Perspective Taking as Egocentric Anchoring and Adjustment', *Journal of Personality and Social Psychology* 87/3 (September 2004): 327–39, https://doi.org/10.1037/0022-3514.87.3.327.
44. Justin L Barrett, *Why Would Anyone Believe in God?* (Walnut Creek, CA: AltaMira Press, 2004).
45. Masahiro Mori, Karl F MacDorman, and Norri Kageki, 'The Uncanny Valley', in *IEEE Robotics and Automation Magazine*, 19/2 (2012): 98–100, https://doi.org/10.1109/MRA.2012.2192811.

Communal Morality

Although AI systems will have different embodiment and moral needs than humans, in the future at least some advanced AI systems will likely interact with humans. For those systems to interact fairly and effectively with humans, they will need to understand human values and needs. As AI systems become more complex and autonomous, it will become increasingly difficult for human developers of AI systems to anticipate the complex ways the systems may respond to diverse interactions. This point has probably already arrived.

In March 23, 2016, Microsoft released a friendly chatbot, called Tay, on Twitter who initially mimicked the language of a nineteen-year-old American girl and learned from interacting with other Twitter users. Within sixteen hours, Microsoft removed Tay from Twitter for making racist, abusive, and sexist tweets. Although a similar chatbot had been used in China since 2014, and Microsoft researchers had partially anticipated some divisive topics with canned responses, Tay was unable to maintain civil public discourse for a full day.[46]

For effective moral interactions, at least four types of knowledge will be required: human understanding of human morality; human understanding of AI morality; AI understanding of human morality; and AI understanding of AI morality. In addition to those logically distinct types of knowledge, more complex interactions will require more sophisticated interpretations.

A theological interpretation of the result of a computer scientist's application of a suite of AI tools on a religious text will differ from a computer scientist's interpretation of the result of a theologian's application of an AI tool on a collection of moral texts. Both would augment human self-understanding but would require different interpretative skills, and the theologian's and computer scientist's investigations would differ. The philosopher of science and technology Shannon Vallor identifies what she calls "technomoral virtues" needed to respond to rapidly developing advanced technology with incompletely understood consequences.[47] She draws upon

---

46. Peter Bright, 'Tay, the Neo-Nazi Millennial Chatbot, Gets Autopsied', Ars Technica, 2016, https://arstechnica.com/information-technology/2016/03/tay-the-neo-nazi-millennial-chatbot-gets-autopsied/.

47. Shannon Vallor, *Technology and the Virtues: A Philosophical Guide to a Future Worth Wanting* (New York: Oxford University Press, 2016), https://doi.org/10.1093/acprof:oso/9780190498511.003.0001.

Aristotelian, Confucian, and Buddhist ethical traditions to characterise shared conceptual resonances, acknowledging the substantial differences between approaches. As humans learn to adapt to emerging technologies, a deeper level of engagement is required when that technology gains the skills humans use for moral and ethical reasoning.

The joint development of human ethics with respect to AI and machine ethics with respect to humans appears a better option than their independent development (or lack of development). For joint development to occur, then AI systems will need to understand human moral and ethical frameworks and the belief systems which structure them. Although possible to learn ethics in a secular context, developing new kinds of ethical principles for a possibly new kind of 'person' would benefit from the background in human religious traditions. For the development to be joint, the AI system also needs to understand toward what humans are striving, and that requires an understanding of spirituality.[48] Machine morality might not require Christian theological understanding *per se* but would require a framework equivalent to theology, such as a revised natural theology, in order to ground moral principles in a coherent anthropology, understand the influence of historical religion on human culture, and identify hopeful human striving in a tragic condition.[49]

Conclusion

Given current AI capacity to analyze and generate theological texts and reasonable assumptions on near-term AI development, it appears AI could learn to read theological texts and make contributions to theological discourse. Depending upon how AI engages society and affects culture, it may become important for AI to gain a theological foundation in order to contribute meaningfully to society and behave morally (or consistent with social moral principles, such as justice).

A harmonious society including humans and AI may require AI to understand humans, even though AI may not need human moral-

---

48. Robert A Emmons, *The Psychology of Ultimate Concerns: Motivation and Spirituality in Personality* (New York: Guilford Press, 1999).
49. Arthur Robert Peacocke, *All That Is : A Naturalistic Faith for the Twenty-First Century*, edited by Philip Clayton (Minneapolis: Fortress Press, 2007).

ity itself, due to its different embodiment, and AI having theological language without foreseeable religious conviction poses a risk. AI already makes decisions affecting human lives and flourishing, and engagement by theologians can contribute to the moral use of technology now, technological enhancement of theological scholarship, and a better understanding of what future AI may require.

Idle Hands and the Omega Point: Labor Automation and Roman Catholic Social Teaching

Levi Checketts

'Scholars of religion and theologians should seriously engage technology because it is empowering humanity in ways that were previously reserved only for gods.'
– Brian Patrick Green[1]

Abstract. The prospect of labor automation raises the question of the role of work in a good Christian life. This article examines three polar theologies of work present in Roman Catholic thought: labor as drudgery, labor as dignified calling and labor as an obstacle. These three theologies inform an eschatological vision of labor—Christians are called to work to build the kingdom of God, not merely to acquire material possessions. Finally, two ultimate issues are raised: the distribution of resources and the problem of idleness in a post-labor world. All of this suggests Catholics must promote a future of dignified labor dedicated to love of neighbor and God.

Key words. Theology of Work, Catholic Social Teaching, Labor Automation, Kingdom of God, Technological Singularity

Bio. Levi Checketts is a Roman Catholic ethicist who teaches at Holy Names University in Oakland and St Mary's College of California in Moraga. He is working on issues related to Catholic ethics of technologies at the intersection of philosophy of technology and Science, Technology and Society (STS) studies. His work has been featured in *Religions*, *Communications Research Trends*, and *Theology and Science* among other publications.

'The Singularity is near!' So proclaimed Ray Kurzweil in 2005. This monumental event is expected to arrive as early as 2045. When it hap-

---

1. Brian Patrick Green, 'The Catholic Church and Technological Progress: Past, Present, and Future', in *Religions* 8:6 (2017): 2–16, at 1; file:///C:/Users/Ted/Downloads/religions-08-00106-v2.pdf.

pens, 'all the changes of the past million years will be superseded by the next five minutes'.[2] The Singularity is the philosopher's stone of the technophiles. It brings with it intelligence beyond compare, both in advancing our own brilliance (Intelligence Amplification, or IA) and in constructing super-powerful artificial intelligences (AI).[3] The benefits of these advancements will play out in our wildest fantasies. Some believe a super-intelligent machine, once fully free to pursue its own aims and amplify and augment its own intelligence, will take its place (if it has not already) as God.[4]

A silicon-based intelligence can always add to itself through hardware extensions and software updates, unlike our limited organic brains, and thus can attain near or total omniscience and omnipotence. The Singularity also promises nigh-immortality as consciousnesses, mapped out as complex patterns, are uploaded into computer substrates, allowing a person who was once a biological organism to continue life as a computer program. Every human biological inadequacy will be outstripped by the mind finally freed from its flesh prison (and installed on a superior silicon replacement).[5] Finally, all physical toil will be obsolete as well: nobody will be required to work in the fields or labor under the sun as robotics and AI take over every necessary job from customers service to manufacturing, from agriculture to law.[6] Every labor required for the survival of the species will

2. Kevin Kelly, 'Technology Doesn't Want a Singularity', in *Singularity 1 on 1*, Singularity Weblog, https://www.singularityweblog.com/kevin-kelly/ (accessed September 18, 2018).

3. Ray Kurzweil, *The Singularity is Near: When Humans Transcend Biology*, PDF e-book edition (New York: Viking, 2005), 135, 194.

4. Lincoln Cannon, 'What is Mormon Transhumanism?', in *Theology and Science*, 13/2 (2015): 212–213. This idea is also alluded to in 'The Singularity Church of the Machine God' in the most recent *Deus Ex* game. This church is apparently a religion designated for machine-augmented human beings, and the 'Machine God' is a super-intelligent being who speaks to the augmented through their brain implants. *Deus Ex: Mankind Divided*, Square Enix, 2016.

5. Hans Moravec, *Mind Children: The Future of Robot and Human Intelligence* (Cambridge, MA: Harvard University Press, 1988), 108–112.

6. Kurzweil, *The Singularity is Near*, 227. It was once thought that the 'professions', those occupations requiring high degree of education and skill, would be safe. However, AI lawyers have already been hired by law firms to replace much of the work attorneys typically do. While an AI lawyer cannot take depositions or represent a client in trial, it can do much of the research lawyers spend their time doing. See: Cecille de Jesus, 'AI Lawyer "Ross" Has Been Hired by Its First

be outsourced to intelligent machines which can both accomplish the task more efficiently and more cheaply than human laborers.

It may come as no surprise that with all the promises the Singularity entails, some scholars have critiqued this view as a 'secular eschatology'.[7] The promise of a new machine god, the belief in silicon-situated afterlife and the promise of a technologically-created paradise have all the markings of Christian beliefs for the end times—absent any strong theological backing.

The promises of AI and IA present themselves as perversions of Christian eschatological tenets. The super-intelligent machine God is the advent of a high-tech idol expressing human desires and understandings rather than the triumphal return of the Son of God. Uploaded consciousness is escapism from death, a refusal to take seriously the condition of human mortality, rather than hope in a restful post-mortal eternal life. Labor automation alone of these three seems not to be obviously theologically problematic. No dogmatic eschatological tenet suggests labor cannot be carried out by machines. Nonetheless, labor automation challenges the meaning of work, an important social issue in Catholic theology. It is my contention that, as an extension of the challenge of social ethics that labor automation entails, it also leads to an eschatological problem for Catholics.

In three of the sections following this, I outline three theologies of work and how they might appraise labor automation. These three approaches see labor, which I define following Hannah Arendt as human activity directed toward consumption or survival,[8] as a curse to fallen humanity, a vocation tied to human dignity, or as an obstacle to overcome on our eschatological journey, respectively. After examining these three, I turn to the connection between labor and the Kingdom of God, wherein lies the connection between techno-optimism and Christian hope. Finally, I conclude by suggesting that achieving wide-scale labor automation changes the social question of just labor to two primary concerns: just distribution and a cure for idleness.

Official Law Firm', in *Futurism*, May 11, 2016 https://futurism.com/artificially-intelligent-lawyer-ross-hired-first-official-law-firm/ (accessed September 18, 2018).

7. See, for example Hava Tirosh-Samuelson, 'Transhumanism as a Secularist Faith', in *Zygon* 47/4 (December 2012): 724–728

8. Hannah Arendt, *The Human Condition*, second edition (Chicago: University of Chicago Press, 1958), 99.

By the Sweat of your Brow: Human Activity Directed toward Consumption and Survival

In the Book of Genesis, the first parents commit the original sin by disobeying God's command to not eat the forbidden fruit. 'By the sweat of your brow you will eat your food until you return to the ground', God impels Adam, condemning humanity to lives of drudgery (Gen 3:19). The reader is led to believe that in the pre-lapsarian state, sustenance was easy-coming and plentiful. The first parents lived simple lives free of the burden of toil. Once sin entered the world, humans were condemned to live frail lives marked primarily by arduous labor for survival.

Thomas Malthus, at the end of *An Essay on the Principle of Population*, argues that God made labor a necessary part of human existence to prevent shiftlessness.[9] Paradisiacal conditions would only encourage humans to lie about enjoying temperate weather while sipping wine, like HG Wells's Eloi of *The Time Machine*. Scarcity, however, forces us to work if we want to eat. This necessity further encourages innovation and industry because craft and guile can reduce our requisite labor. Thus, Malthus goes on to argue, the wealth of the Industrial Revolution cannot, and should not, be equally distributed, for this will only encourage idle behavior. God has ordained human beings to work for their food, thus imposing both a 'carrot and stick' method where hard work is rewarded with material blessings but laziness leads us to starvation.

Jacques Ellul, on a somewhat different tack, argues that the fall leads to human beings needing *technique*, or the use of technological tools, to wrest from the earth the resources needed for survival.[10] The struggle of mortality requires human beings to employ industry, including both the labor of their hands and the cleverness of their minds, to survive. In the post-lapsarian world, *technique* becomes the instrument by which humanity takes dominion over the earth, asserting ourselves as rulers rather than caretakers.[11] This new relation sets

---

9. Thomas R Malthus, *An Essay on the Principle of Population* (London: J Johnson, 1798), 113.
10. Jacques Ellul, 'Technique and the Opening Chapters of Genesis', in *Theology and Technology: Essays in Christian Analysis and Exegesis*, edited by Carl Mitcham and Jim Grote (Lanham: University Press of America, 1984), 131.
11. Jacques Ellul, 'The Relationship between Man and Creation in the Bible', in Mitcham and Grote, 140.

humanity in antagonistic relation to the natural world. We exploit and destroy for our survival, yet the life of labor is, to paraphrase Hobbes, 'nasty, brutish and short'. Nature and humanity compete, and *technique* grants humans the possibility of gaining the upper hand, but always within the context of a tenuous order maintained by violence.

Thus, according to the Malthusian-Ellulian view, labor is an effect of the fall. Humanity's original sin is the source of the need for labor. If Adam and Eve had obeyed God's command, we would live free from drudgery. The world we actually live in, however, is one where we both toil and die as a result of sin. Labor can be mitigated, but never abolished. We can employ our tools to lighten the load, but the violence of nature can only be staved off, never vanquished in this life. In the end, even the best medical and labor-saving technologies fail as illness and old age inevitably bring death.

How does this view consider labor obsolescence? On the one hand, labor automation may be impossible fully, as human beings, by metaphysical design, *must* be engaged in earnest labor or otherwise must die. On the other hand, the society where labor has freed all hands may lead to a society of human stagnation as nothing propels human excellence. We suffer the fate of Friedrich Nietzsche's 'last men' who claim "'We have discovered happiness,'" . . . and blink thereby'.[12] This fate is comparable to limbo: we do not experience suffering or torment, but neither do we experience the joys or triumphs of a life well lived.

This particular theology of work held sway in Medieval Catholicism. Max Weber notes that pre-modern Catholic attitudes toward labor saw it as essentially a baser task opposed to the higher callings of the ascetic life.[13] Those who would pursue the more spiritual (and, by extension, more sanctified) must leave behind the 'worldly' tasks of normal human labor. Indeed, labor was seen as a degrading condition, unfit for the truly Christian, in the Middle Ages, and its value only lay in its potential for sustenance.[14] This view is totally aban-

12. Friedrich Nietzsche, *Thus Spake Zarathustra: A Book for All and None*, translated by Thomas Common, Amazon Kindle e-book edition (Houston: Everlasting Flames Publishing, 2010), 'Zarathustra's Prologue', 5.
13. Max Weber, *The Protestant Ethic and the 'Spirit' of Capitalism, and Other Writings*, edited and translated by Peter Baehr and Gordon C Wells (New York: Penguin Books, 2002), 25.
14. Arendt, *The Human Condition*, 317–318.

doned in contemporary Catholic theology, and perhaps no current
Catholic theology of labor sees work as connected to sin and death.
Indeed, modern Catholic theology, as illustrated below, tends to see
labor as a dignified pursuit and rest from labor a worthy reward.

The Laborer is Worthy of His Hire: a Vocation tied to Human Dignity

The view most prominent within the Catholic Tradition today is that
work has an important place within the concept of human dignity.
Labor is not punishment for sin, but a life-fulfilling function by which
we draw closer to God. Work becomes a fulfillment of God's expectations of us on earth—a 'calling' in the sense of Luther and broader
Protestant theology.[15] Rather than see labor as the consequence of
fall, this view sees it as a genuinely human—and genuinely Christian—task that draws us nearer to our fellow human beings, to the
earth, and to God.

Human beings, according to Pope John Paul II, have a 'universal
calling' to work because it is through work that we become like God
by taking dominion of the earth.[16] In this view, God's call to humanity
in Genesis 1:28 to 'subdue the earth' re-orients the seemingly punitive
nature of God's words in Genesis 3:19. The ominous 'sweat of your
brow' becomes the means by which we imitate God, not the curse of
a fallen humanity. The pontiff goes on to say, 'Work is a good thing for
[the human being]—a good thing for his humanity—because through
work [the human] *not only transforms nature*, adapting it to his own
needs, but he also *achieves fulfilment* as a human being and indeed,
in a sense, becomes "more a human being".'[17] This is the genuinely
human task we are called to. As God is active through creative work
in the universe, and human beings are made in the image of God, we
fulfill our divinely-given mandate through working like God.[18]

---

15. Weber, *The Protestant Ethic and the 'Spirit' of Capitalism*, 29.
16. John Paul II, *Laborem Exercens* (Vatican City: Libreria Editrice Vaticana, 1981),
    9.
17. John Paul II, *Laborem Exercens*. Emphases original.
18. *Cf* The Second Vatican Council, *Gadium et Spes: The Pastoral Constitution of the
    Church in the Modern World* (Vatican City: Libreria Editrice Vaticana, 1965), 34;
    Paul VI, *Populorum Progressio* (Vatican City: Libreria Editrice Vaticana, 1967),
    27.

A positive theology of work is critical when work becomes exploitative or demeaning. In the first Catholic social encyclical, Pope Leo XIII reminds employers that 'according to natural reason and Christian philosophy, working for gain is creditable, not shameful, to a [person], since it enables him to earn an honorable livelihood; but to misuse [people] as though they were things in the pursuit of gain, or to value them solely for their physical powers—that is truly shameful and inhuman.'[19] This sentiment is likewise echoed in *Gaudium et Spes* (27), *Populorum Progressio* (28), *Quadragesimo Anno* (83) and in other magisterial documents. The abuse or cheapening of laborers is morally repugnant and is a violation of their dignity; it exploits the means by which human beings both survive and imitate their Creator. Catholic leaders therefore call on employers to provide dignified conditions for their workers and on states to create legal protections against exploitation.[20] Work must therefore be protected because of its central function in a dignified human life.

This view is most prominent across Catholic social teaching because work plays an important function in human social activity. Work is necessary for the support of families.[21] Work allows parents to provide for children, the elderly and disabled within the family unit. The importance of care and familial responsibility requires access to dignified labor. Additionally, work builds up comradery among workers for at least two reasons. First, cooperation brings a feeling of solidarity as workers strive to achieve shared goals.[22] Second, cooperative action allows a compounding of benefits as labor specialisation yields an increase of productivity, providing a natural benefit for all who engage in shared labor.[23] For this reason, workers unions and associations are typically good.[24] Finally, work contributes to the broader common good both because it allows people to

---

19. Leo XIII, *Rerum Novarum* (Vatican City: Libreria Editrice Vaticana, 1891), 20.
20. John XXIII, *Mater et Magistra* (Vatican City: Libreria Editrice Vaticana, 1961), 21; Pius XI, *Quadragesimo Anno* (Vatican City: Libreria Editrice Vaticana, 1931), 28.
21. John Paul II, *Laborem Exercens*, 10.
22. Vatican II, *Gadium et Spes*, 68.
23. John XXIII, *Mater et Magistra*, 60.
24. See: Leo XIII, *Rerum Novarum*, 48; John Paul II, *Laborem Exercens*, 20; Vatican II, *Gadium et Spes*, 68; Paul VI, 38.

contribute to the well-being of society and because it allows the able-bodied to aid their fellows who are unable to work.[25]

Thus, a general Catholic social theology of work is as follows. Work affirms human dignity by fostering solidarity between workers, providing for the common good, and, ontologically, imitating the creative activity of God. Human beings ought to have meaningful and fulfilling work allowing them to meet their personal and familial needs. Working conditions which prevent willing workers from finding work, which alienate or mechanize human labor, which create unsafe or hostile environments, or which underpay employees for their labor are affronts to human dignity. Dignified work is of central importance for social commutations; expressed biblically, 'The laborer is worthy of his hire' (Lk 10:7, KJV).

The situation of automated technology becomes problematic from a Catholic social perspective for various reasons. The first and most obvious is that it deprives people of the dignity inherent in labor. Those unable to find jobs because of automation will be left feeling undignified because they lose the ability to exercise the call to be like God, to further the common good, or even to create something that reflects their unique gifts from God.[26] Moreover, those able to retain employment, such as those hired to supervise machines, will feel a decreased sense of solidarity and connectedness to their fellows, many of whom lack work. God has made us to live and work within community, not as isolated drones. Finally, as I discuss further below, dignified work allows men and women to achieve flourishing; lack of work may lead to resource deprivation.

They neither Toil nor Spin: an Obstacle to Overcome on our Eschatological Journey

In Luke 12 and Matthew 6, Jesus counsels his disciples to put off worries about their material necessities. Jesus reminds his disciples, situated as they are in an agrarian society, that other living things like sparrows and lilies do not labor yet are sustained. They should take a lesson from these creatures; Jesus counsels them, 'Seek first [God's] kingdom and [God's] righteousness, and all these things will be given

---

25. John XXIII, *Mater et Magistr*, 78–81.
26. See, for example, Edward C Vacek, *Love, Human and Divine: the Heart of Christian Ethics* (Washington: Georgetown University Press, 1994), 252.

to you as well' (Matt 6:33 NIV). Thus, Jesus opens the possibility for a life lived independent of labor.

The Bible does not advocate strongly for a cessation of labor, but there are hints occasionally that God's mercy will be manifest in rest from drudgery. In Exodus 3:17, God promises to bring Israel out of Egypt into 'a land flowing with milk and honey'. The slavery of Egypt is contrasted against a paradise of seemingly plentiful food and minimal labor. In Revelation 21, God promises to 'wipe every tear from their eyes' in the new world where the peoples of all nations devote themselves solely to worship of God in the New Jerusalem. Ordinary suffering and labor are replaced by twenty-four-hour worship. Both the Book of Isaiah and the Gospel of Matthew promise spiritual, though not physical, relief from the burdens of labor. Isaiah 55 promises satisfaction to the hungry, and Matthew 11 promises rest to the weary.

Clearly the biblical authors' audiences saw value in a life absent of toil. One may even read the sabbath as God's providential illustration for an eventual cessation of labor. In all of this, we read a yearning of biblical authors and promise for rest for those whose labors and toils are burdensome. If work is ordinarily good in the dominant Catholic social worldview, a final theology of work suggests the life of the Christian ought to be other than back-breaking labor in the fields.

This view is most in agreement with the promise of automated labor. Machines to do the most dangerous, difficult, dull, disrespected or dirty labor humans currently do amounts to emancipation from these affronts to human dignity. The 'cog in the machine' metaphor of industrialized labor, popularized by Charlie Chaplin's *Modern Times*, illustrates the disparity between the dignified work Catholic social teaching praises and the reality of many laborers in industrialized nations. The suffering of women and children in sweatshops and the suffering of Hebrew slaves in Egypt both cry out for deliverance from drudgery. Why should we not allow God to work to alleviate this suffering through technology today as God did through the Exodus then?

The Jesuit mystic and paleontologist Pierre Teilhard de Chardin is perhaps the clearest Catholic supporter of this prospect. He addresses the question of technological unemployment in his writings. 'Economists are horrified by the growing number of idle hands',[27] he notes, because of the economic problem of the survival of thousands or millions of people lacking paid work. But, Teilhard assures us, this unemployment 'heralds the release of spiritual energy—every pair of hands freed means a brain freed for thought'.[28] Teilhard sees intellectual freedom won by technological unemployment as an evolutionary step. While this 'trait' of humanity seems unfit at the moment—without suitable employment, people will die—it will ultimately prove to be a fitter trait because humanity will become more intellectually oriented than physically dependent.

The possibility of pursuing greater advances in science, technology, exploration, art, philosophy or other forms of thought constitutes an increasing of the 'psychic temperature' of the earth.[29] This increasing of psychic temperature is part of Teilhard's understanding of the necessary movement for achieving the 'Omega Point', an eschatological destiny Teilhard sees as the goal of evolution, and which he refers to in more theological writings as humanity becoming 'cosmic Christ'.[30] In other words, Teilhard sees technological unemployment as a necessary step whereby human beings are able to more fully devote themselves to those intellectual pursuits which will help us achieve our eschatological goal and becoming one with a converging universe.

Other Roman Catholics, especially Jesuits, have written in a similar vein. Teilhard's disciple, Wilhelm Fudpucker, argues that the "universal and egalitarian state free from want and fear" characteristic of Christian eschatological visions entails the pro-social use of new technologies to Christian ends.[31] André Malet argues technologies should be used to fulfill the works of mercy Christ prescribes in Matthew 25,

---

27. Pierre Teilhard de Chardin, *The Future of Man*, translated by Norman Denny (New York: Double Day, 1964), 166.
28. Pierre Teilhard de Chardin, *Activation of Energy: Enlightening Reflections on Spiritual Energy*, translated by René Hague (San Diego: Harcourt, Inc, 1978), 160.
29. Pierre Teilhard de Chardin, *Man's Place in Nature: The Human Zoological Group*, translated by René Hague (London: Fontana, 1966), 98.
30. Pierre Teilhard de Chardin, *Science and Christ*, translated by René Hague (New York: Harper & Row, 1965), 54.
31. Wilhelm F Fudpucker, 'Through Technological Christianity to Christian Technology', in Mitcham and Grote, 59, 65.

including feeding, clothing, sheltering and assisting our fellows.[32] W Norris Clarke endorses the use of technology to overcome our physical limitations, including our bodily frailties and limitations, to free our souls for higher purposes.[33] Each of these views seems to suggest technology should be used to lessen human dependence on human labor for our survival. Technology allows us to help those who cannot otherwise work, to free ourselves for higher work, and to establish a world free from suffering and want. Thus, a different reading of Catholic thought suggests technological unemployment, assuming it serves to advance the common good,[34] is a worthy endeavor.

The Harvest is Ready but the Laborers are Few: More on Eschatology

These theologies of labor give us useful material to reflect on, but, aside from the Teilhardian view, say nothing about labor in the eschaton. At present, however, automation is a question of future happenings; the goal of proponents of automation is a future free from drudgery contrary to the present situation of arduous work. This is an eschatological vision—the end they see for humanity is one where tedium and toil are minimised if not fully eliminated. The mind will finally be free from irksome physical necessities to pursue whatever life it sees fit.[35] I have argued elsewhere that the critical questions of technological ethics are questions of consequences, and the guiding moral principle for Christians must be eschatological.[36] This fact

---

32. André Malet, 'The Believer in the Presence of Technique', in Mitcham and Grote, 105.
33. W Norris Clarke, 'Technology and Man: A Christian View', in *Technology and Philosophy: Readings in the Philosophical Problems of Technology*, edited by Carl Mitcham and Robert Mackey (New York: The Free Press, 1972), 249.
34. As should be evident by now, the common good is a key idea in much of Catholic moral theology. It is often misconstrued as some sort of utilitarian principle of benefitting the majority, but Thomas Aquinas clarifies it as '*universal* happiness'. Universal is not the same as majority, so an advancement that benefits *many* people but disadvantages *a few* is not truthfully an advancement of the common good. Thomas Aquinas, *Summa Theologiae*, Prima pars Secundae partis Question 90, Article 2, emphasis mine.
35. Kurzweil, *The Singularity is Near*, 32.
36. Levi Checketts, *Homo Gubernator: A Moral Anthropology for New Technologies*, PhD dissertation (The Graduate Theological Union, Berkeley, CA, January 31, 2018), 260.

holds true for automated labor just as much as consciousness uploading, genetic engineering or super-intelligent AI. In other words, *the
moral issue at hand is the place of labor in the Christian eschaton,*
and we must compare this vision with the goals of labor automation.

Within the biblical narrative, Jesus advises a different form of
labor for the coming kingdom of God. In both Matthew 10 and Luke
10, Jesus sends out his disciples to preach the Gospel around Galilee,
admonishing them to receive the charity of those who believe rather
than selling their services. Likewise, in Matthew 9:37, in reference to
the difficulty of 'preaching the good news of the kingdom' and other
forms of ministry, Jesus notes that 'the harvest is great but the laborers are few', suggesting that Jesus's model of ministry is a call to labor.
At the end of the Gospels of Matthew (28:16–20) and Mark (16:15–
18), Jesus's parting words to his disciples is the Great Commission,
sending them as messengers to the world to witness of his life and
ministry. In each of these pericopes, Jesus uses notions of labor and
work in a different sense from ordinary means-to-survive. The labor
Jesus requires of his disciples, at least in certain parts of the gospels, is
a labor of ministry to others and not back-breaking toil in the fields.

This idea finds resonance in the notion of 'kingdom building' articulated by several social theologians of the twentieth century. Both Catholic and Protestant theologians, including Walter
Rauschensbusch, Martin Luther King, Jr, Johann-Baptist Metz and
Gustavo Gutierrez, contest that the Christian must be active today,
not in securing his or her own salvation, but in working to establish
God's kingdom here on earth.[37] One even finds in more traditional
theologians, including Karl Rahner and John Paul II, an emphasis
on Christians' moral obligation to put their energies into working
together with God for the sake of God's kingdom.[38] In the view of

---

37. Walter Rauschenbusch, *A Theology for the Social Gospel* (New York: Cosimo
    Classics, 2012), 133; Martin Luther King, Jr, 'Letter from Birmingham City Jail',
    A Testament of Hope: The Essential Writings of Martin Luther King, Jr, edited by
    James Melvin Washington (San Francisco: Harper & Row, 1986), 296; Jonhannes
    B Metz, *Theology of the World,* translated by William Glen-Doepel (New York:
    Herder & Herder, 1969), 94; Gustavo Gutierrez, *A Theology of Liberation,* trans.
    Caridad Inda and John Eagleston (Maryknoll: Orbis Books, 1973), 103.
38. Karl Rahner, 'Notes on the Lay Apostolate', *Man in the Church,* Theological
    Investigations, Volume 2, translated Karl Kruger (Baltimore: Helicon Press,
    1963), 323; John Paul II, 'All Are Called to Build God's Kingdom' (General
    Audience), December 6, 2000.

these theologians, the Christian call to labor is primarily one of carrying out those works that are at their heart most Christian: spreading the Gospel, carrying out the works of mercy, praising God through word and deed, praying without ceasing, working for peace and justice in the world, and overall creating a society that reflects the eschatological vision we hold.

The theological turn to eschatology becomes especially important in an industrialised world. In a world where future-oriented thinking, especially in science and technology, has become the norm, Metz recognises that the Church must be futurally oriented as well; 'the hope which the Christian faith has in regard to the future cannot be realised independently of the world and its future, [and] this hope must answer, must be responsible for, the one promised future and hence also for the future of the world'.[39] The proper Christian reaction to new technologies is not knee-jerk resistance, but rather appraisal through the lens of eschatological achievement. Even with respect to a technology as sensitive as biological engineering, Karl Rahner noted the critical moral question was whether such a technology can prepare the way for God's kingdom by facilitating better love of neighbor.[40] In the particular context of work, Teilhard notes that the advantage of technological unemployment is it allows more people to be engaged in research.[41] However, he also notes that human progress 'is not a *tête-à-tête* or a *corps-à-corps* . . . it is a heart-to-heart', which 'can achieve its consummation only in becoming Christianized'.[42] The necessary direction of evolution, even if self-directed, is, for Teilhard, 'upward and forward'—attentive to both material advancement and spiritual perfection.[43] Thus, an important consideration raised by these theologians is that the essential issue at hand should not be whether automation of labor accords with a good theology of work, but rather whether it aligns with our eschatological understandings.

On this front, we see that automation of labor, at least as presented by Kurzweil and others, is incompatible with Christian theology. The

39. Metz, *Theology of the World*, 91.
40. Karl Rahner, 'The Experiment with Man', in *Theological Investigations* Volume IX, translated by Graham Harrison (London: Darton, Longman & Todd, 1972), 220–221.
41. Teilhard, *Future of Man*, 167.
42. Teilhard, *Future of Man*, 67.
43. Teilhard, *Future of Man*, 265–269.

Singularitarian vision of automation of labor is rooted in materialist conceptions of happiness and life-fulfillment. Capitalism, with its focus on efficiency and reduction of costs, moves logically toward the goal of perfect mechanical operation. Laboring machines will be able to do greater amounts of work for extended periods of time with fractions of the cost of human laborers. We humans, then, are freed finally to enjoy the fruits of a life purchased by our ingenuity. The aim of this endeavor, to achieve a materialistic paradise, is paradoxical: through application of the capitalist values of industry and innovation, one is able to finally escape the conditions that require these virtues. So much for virtue being its own reward! But here one finds the final obstacle: once the need for labor is eliminated, we will be left with the unanswered problem of lives devoid of ultimate meaning.[44] Christianity, for its part, has already positively answered the challenge left by automation, and its response is that we are called to be actively building the Kingdom of God. This means that the project of removing labor for the sake of a life of infinite leisure is contrary to the Christian's understanding of the place of work within the purpose of life. Each of the three above theologies of work contends that the Catholic is not called to work merely to put bread on the table. The Catholic social teaching view sees labor as a dignified path for humanity, and both the first and third views see labor as a hindrance to lives lived pursuing higher callings, through other forms of work. Our activity is therefore not measured by its efficiency or material yield, but rather on its expression of love of God and neighbor and its dedication to a life lived in service of God. Because the Christian understands labor not as a burden, but rather as her calling whereby she cooperates with God and neighbor within the Kingdom of God, her aims in work must be other than the aims the Singularitarians espouse. The leisurely eschatology of labor automation is not the loving eschatology of the Kingdom of God.

Two Final Issues

Theologies of work provide helpful guidelines today for how to think of the labor we are asked to perform and the labor we ask others to

---

44. See, for example, Hans Jonas, *The Phenomenon of Life: Towards a Philosophical Biology* (New York: Dell Publishing Co, 1966), 209

perform. Work conceived as curse, dignified calling or surmountable obstacle changes our conception of our responsibility in working or eliminating work. However, while these theologies inform Christian attitudes toward labor, it is unlikely that the those pushing for technological unemployment will carefully consider them. A new report from the World Economic Forum on jobs and automation brings to light several problems of automation, including widening gaps between rich and poor or employed and unemployed, but optimistically suggests workers will be 'reskilled' or 'augmented' in their work.[45] Nonetheless, the report also surmises that as soon as 2022, up to fifty per cent of jobs across industries will experience reduction due to automation.[46] One can extrapolate that this trend will continue, especially in those occupations considered 'labor'. As such, an important final consideration is the question of what to do *when* labor becomes obsolete. With the question of inevitability and not merely possibility of technological unemployment, two important final issues reveal themselves: the problem of distribution and the problem of idle hands.

'*Cui bono?*' Lucius Cassius used to ask of criminals—who benefits? We might in turn ask who benefits from the automation of labor. It is clear that the greatest benefit will fall to those who control the machinery or the means of production. The bourgeoisie Marx railed against in the early nineteenth century pale in threat to a class who forgoes alienating the workers by eliminating them. It is unlikely that the members of the working class, or even those in middle class occupations subject to automation, will benefit dramatically from labor automation. The elimination of most need for human labor means the elimination of most forms of human employment.

Of course, in a capitalist economy, producers require a market to make profit. If Apple Computers or Toyota Automotive can be reduced to a handful of executives and engineers, they still need people buying their products to make money. As a result, one of three things is likely. First, the entrepreneurially-minded unemployed may find new possibilities for work, including new occupations and new industries, as suggested by both Malthus and the WEF. Indeed,

---

45. World Economic Forum, *The Future of Jobs Report 2018* (Geneva: World Economic Forum, 2018), 3.
46. World Economic Forum, *The Future of Jobs Report 2018*, 16.

optimistic attitudes toward technological unemployment assume as much will happen.[47] Second, some sort of universal basic income may be established to ensure that the unemployed masses still have means to survive—and further contribute to the capitalistic structures in place. Finally, corporations may invent menial and degrading forms of labor, such as riding a stationary bike to generate electricity,[48] in order to take advantage of the newly unemployed and desperate.[49]

All of this, of course, ignores the problem of those living outside of industrialised nations. As much as we may decry labor rights violations of factory workers in developing countries, their sudden unemployment does not promise a much better outcome. Consider the case of Foxconn, a company that had been criticized for its subhuman conditions in factories in China a few years ago. Today, they solve this problem by promoting mass unemployment through replacing laborers with machines.[50] Will consumer-goods producing corporations like Nike and Apple ensure the well-being of former sweatshop workers displaced by automation? Will the current global inequality be exacerbated when people of the 'third world' become cut off from possibilities of acquiring wealth because industrialized nations have automated processes that create better and cheaper goods than human workers ever could?

Roman Catholic social ethics provides an unequivocal response to this problem. Labor automation must not result in widespread destitution. While Catholic social teaching has always remained wary of socialist solutions, especially communism, it has also always raised a critical voice against capitalist systems that leave people impover-

---

47. See: Ray Kurzweil, 'Progress and Relinquishment', in *The Transhumanist Reader: Classical and Contemporary Essays on the Science, Technology and Philosophy of the Human Future*, edited by Max More and Natasha Vita-More (Malden, MA: Wiley-Blackwell, 2013), 458.

48. See, for example, the science fiction television episode 'Fifteen Million Merits', in *Black Mirror*, Series 1, ep. 2.

49. It is also possible all three of these scenarios play out. A UBI may be low enough to meet 'essential costs' as defined by governmental agencies, but may push men and women to seek out further income through entrepreneurial endeavors or menial labor.

50. Nick Statt 'iPhone Manufacturer Foxconn Planns to Replace almost Every Human Worker with Robots', in *The Verge* December 30, 2016 https://www. theverge.com/2016/12/30/14128870/foxconn-robots-automation-apple-iphone-china-manufacturing (accessed September 22, 2018).

ished. Catholicism will need to raise a strong and loud voice to ensure that as labor automation is pursued, just distribution of the fruits of automation is also pursued. Technological 'progress' at the expense of millions or billions of people's survival is morally untenable.

'Idle hands are the devil's workshop' (Prov 16:27 TLB). The other problem related to labor automation is the fundamental problem of unemployment, that is, lack of occupation for those millions or billions replaced by machines. Many religious figures have advocated hard work as a prophylactic against vices like fornication, alcoholism, drug abuse, gambling or theft.[51] Whether or not this advice is sound, the problem remains—if people are not 'occupied' with labor, with what will they be occupied?

The less palatable option, as illustrated in science fiction stories, including the recent Steven Spielberg-directed *Ready Player One*, is a world of idleness. People will engage, not in constructive efforts, but in time-wasting pursuits, such as binge-watching television shows or devoting hours to massive multiplayer online video games, getting high or drunk, scrolling mindlessly through millions of pages of hypertext on the Internet, committing small acts of violence as 'harmless pranks' for entertainment, engaging in other high-risk behaviors 'for the thrill', and so forth. Twentieth century capitalism has not provided us with any confidence that it can supply life meaning. The eschatological vision of Singularitarianism is challenged by cultural movements like existentialism and postmodernism, and time-wasting distractions like television, social media and video games. A future with no work is not a guarantee for a future of fulfilled lives.

The task for Catholics is clear enough; they should be engaged in the work of co-constructing the kingdom of God. Whether that means through ordained ministry, through proselytizing, through art, through writing, through service ministries, or another means of actively serving God and neighbor will depend on what the believer feels called to and what needs are most pressing. At present, there is no shortage of need for: people working for economic, racial, sexual and environmental justice; people witnessing against harmful or

---

51. See, for example Leo XIII, *Rerum Novarum*, 28; Robert Owen, 'Report to the Committee for the Relief of the Manufacturing Poor', in *A New View of Society and Other Writings* (London: Dent, 1966), 160; James Adderley, 'Social Aspects of the Gospel', in *Vox Clamantium: The Gospel of the People*, edited by Andrew Reid (London: William Clowes and Sons, 1894), 102.

destructive policies and programs; theologians thoughtfully engaging with new technologies, new sciences and other new disciplines; scientists, engineers and other scholars seeking to glorify God through their work; artists, musicians, writers and videographers praising God through various media; liturgists who understand the needs of worship communities; politicians, lawyers and judges working to protect the common good; doctors, nurses, therapists and others who heal body and mind; teachers who raise up new generations in wisdom and love. We also have great needs for manual labor, including in home construction, agricultural production and custodial maintenance, though these necessities may be obsolete with new automation. Regardless, the kingdom of God now requires, and will yet require, many active laborers, devoting their time, talents and energy to God and neighbor.

Idleness in the broader society may be a worse problem. While a good Christian may devote his life to pastoral care for the sick or elderly, painting icons, or writing hymns, it is unclear what the rest of the population will do. Certainly, some will still pursue worthy causes such as science, artistic expression or philanthropic endeavors, but many will undoubtedly turn to idleness. The failures of communism, or even Robert Owen's socialist commune 'New Harmony', are evidence of the problems of human laziness. In a sense, Malthus is vindicated; the necessity of work provides the motivation to work. To those unemployed masses who choose violence, or vice, the Christian has a special mission. Evangelisation, character reform and addiction recovery have been critical Christian ministries for centuries and will undoubtedly continue in the post-labor future. No missionary to the pagans will be able to convince all—that is the work of Christ after all—but we laborers in the vineyard need to do our part.

Conclusion

As John Lennon said, 'Everything will be ok in the end. If it's not ok, it's not the end'. We Christians wait in joyful hope for the promised kingdom of God, where every tear will be dried and every misery relieved. Since the eighteenth century, the relationship between labor and machinery has been the subject of great energy among the socially conscious, including Robert Owen, Karl Marx, Friedrich Engels, John Ruskin, Lord Byron, Walter Rauschenbusch, Hannah Arendt, Herbert Marcuse, Nikolai Berdyaev, and many Catholic theologians and popes, as noted above. The promise of fully automated labor does not solve this question; it complicates the issue by adding new dimensions and new problems to it. These new questions will require flexible and informed responses as they arise. We can anticipate some appropriate responses, but ultimately the same sort of social reflection characteristic of Catholic social thought reaching back to the mid-nineteenth century will be needed as new socio-technical-economic realities come to light.[52] Among those stances which seem to be foundational to Catholic social thought, even in the age of labor automation, are questions of just resource distribution and dignified work for all.

---

52. Contrary to popular belief, *Rerum Novarum* was not the beginning of Catholic social thought; rather it was the beginning of *magisterial* Catholic social thought. Earlier movements such as the Fribourg Union and the work of Wilhelm Ketteler laid the foundation for later development in CST. See: Normand J Paulhus, 'Social Catholicism and the Fribourg Union', in *Selected Papers from the Annual Meeting of the Society for Christian Ethics*, 21 (1980): 63–88.

CPSIA information can be obtained
at www.ICGtesting.com
Printed in the USA
BVHW072037301219
568186BV00001B/42/P